HARDWARE BILLIONAIRES

Why Read This book?

Dive into the world of innovation and creation with 'Hardware Billionaires.' This indispensable guide is a compass for daring hardware creators, visionary entrepreneurs, and anyone with a product dream waiting to break free from their imagination. With a wealth of 25 insider tips and a treasure trove of real-life experiences, this book is your roadmap to transforming your ideas into awe-inspiring products that captivate the market.

Author Jason Lam, a native of Silicon Valley's beating heart in San Francisco, has lived the trials and triumphs of a drone designer in a realm where hardware startups faced skepticism from even the most steadfast investors. Witnessing the rise and fall of hardware ventures that secured millions in capital, only to falter within two years, Lam emerged from this crucible with invaluable insights. Years of perseverance, marked by both failures and victories, led him to the creation of IDOLCAM, a journey he now chronicles to illuminate the path for others in the struggles of electronic product development.

In 'Hardware Billionaires,' Lam's narrative encapsulates the entirety of his undertaking, from humble beginnings with a mere few hundred dollars, through the countless obstacles, to the triumphant unveiling of IDOLCAM, a cutting-edge, intricately designed video camera. Drawn from firsthand encounters, his revelations are like a mentor's guidance, capable of saving millions in product development costs and expediting your journey to market entry. Beyond the mechanics of creation, the book delves into marketing, branding, crowdfunding, and even explores the often-overlooked realms of mindset, spirituality, and eCommerce intricacies.

Unlock consultant-level insights encapsulated within these pages. 'Hardware Billionaires' isn't just a guide, it's an odyssey through the highs and lows of turning concepts into product empires. Let this book be your cornerstone to chart your course, steer past pitfalls, and emerge not just as a creator, but as a conqueror of the world of hardware innovation. Your journey from idea to empire starts here.

Turn Your Idea Into A Product Empire.

About the Author, Jason Lam

Hailing from the vibrant epicenter of innovation, Silicon Valley, Jason Lam embodies the spirit of a modern Renaissance figure. With a multifaceted journey that seamlessly weaves through art, technology, and entrepreneurial prowess, Lam's life is a testament to his relentless pursuit of pushing boundaries.

Commencing his career as a visionary New York fashion photographer, Lam's creative lens captured the essence of iconic brands like Coca-Cola, America's Top Model, and Pepsi, etching his name among the industry's luminaries. His innate ability to infuse life into every frame laid the foundation for his odyssey into uncharted territories.

Fueled by an unquenchable curiosity, Lam's fascination with fly RC helicopters unfurled a new chapter. As if guided by destiny, he embarked on a path of inventiveness that led to the birth of his groundbreaking concept, a flying camera. Even before the drone era dawned, Lam's audacious experimentation gave birth to a flying camera prototype, catapulting him into the league of visionaries who redefine the realm of possibilities.

As a true pioneer of innovative hardware, Lam's journey took yet another transformative turn. A journey that began with his love for capturing beauty blossomed into the creation of IDOLCAM, a revolutionary all-in-one video camera solution meticulously crafted for the dynamic needs of content creators. Seamlessly encapsulating cutting-edge technology and user-centric design, IDOLCAM transcends the conventional, empowering creators to paint their narratives with unprecedented versatility and brilliance.

Lam's legacy radiates not merely from his innovations, but from his relentless spirit and tenacity. He is the embodiment of a trailblazer who defies conventions, seamlessly navigating between diverse disciplines, and creating an indelible impact at every juncture. Beyond the accolades and accomplishments, his journey exemplifies the power of unbridled passion in sculpting the trajectory of one's life.

In a world that yearns for fresh perspectives and groundbreaking ideas, Jason Lam stands as a beacon, a true luminary who sparks inspiration and drives transformation. His life story serves as a reminder that the human spirit knows no bounds when fueled by the fusion of creativity, technology, and unwavering determination.

HARDWARE BILLIONAIRES

Turn your idea into a Product Empire.

A guide for resources lacking Hardware Creators to crack the Hardware code.

Written by,

Jason Lam

From the founder of IDOLCAM, taking you into his impossible journey of creating a world class video camera on a shoestring budget.

IDOLCAM,

FROM CONCEPT TO PRODUCTION.

UNRAVELING THE SECRETS BEHIND

HARDWARE CREATION.

Get "Hardware Billionaires" book at,

https://www.idolcam.co/hardwarebillionaires.html

Hardware Billionaires

Turn your idea into a Product Empire.

Jason Lam

ALL RIGHTS ARE RESERVED.

No permission is given for any part of this book to be reproduced, transmitted in any form or means; electronic or mechanical, stored in a retrieval system, photocopied, recorded, scanned, or otherwise. Any of these actions require the proper written permission of the author.

ISBN: 979-8-218-27205-0

IDOLCAM Co. Publishing

support@Idolcam.co

www.IDOLCAM CO

TABLE OF CONTENTS

Preface 11
Intro
   Are you ready? 13
Chapter 1
   How it all begins 22
Chapter 2
   The Magical City 56
Chapter 3
   Kickstarter Funding 71
Chapter 4
   Pre-Order Funding 82
Chapter 5
   Production Process 95
Chapter 6
   Cash flow, Key to Survival 112
Chapter 7
   OEM & ODM 122
Chapter 8
   Growth Marketing 128

Chapter 9
    Branding for Profit..138
Chapter 10
    Timing, the X Factor 144
Chapter 11
    Confidence & Mental Toughness 150
Chapter 12
    Big Idea & Hobbies...159
Chapter 13
    Tactics & Strategies...171
Chapter 14
    Spirituality & Health..176
Chapter 15
    The Next Hardware Billionaire 182
Chapter 16
    Final Words 184

Preface

There are so many creatives, tinkerers and hobbyists out there with great ideas about how a product they often use should have been designed instead of their current stale form and features. However, the leap from the ideation to realization is often too wide of a gap for most people to tackle. I had my first idea of a device that could track my keychain and wallet while I was 18 years old because I often spend 20 minutes looking for them, which is what the company Tile, or the better known brand Apple Air-tag has done after 20 years. At the time, I saw an invention development company's ad constantly playing on TV calling for inventors with new ideas. Being naive as I was, I picked up the phone and told them my idea of a key tracker and they replied over the phone that I need to send them $800 to begin the process and that stopped me from proceeding as a young hardware entrepreneur. Many years later, in my late twenties, serendipity got me back in hardware creation. Until now, electronic Hardware are mysterious to most solo creators and often a long, expensive and complex process. My hope with this book is to share with you my hardware failures, triumph, tips and experience on how you can turn your amazing product idea into real products for a lot less money, time and a shot at one day turning it into a billion dollar empire.

Jason Lam
IDOLCAM Founder

Intro

Are you ready?

Wait, stop, you should really stop reading this book and slowly close the cover. You still have time to save yourself from years of pain and misery. Better to walk away now and live a normal life like everyone else because this journey you are about to embark on would require strong will and determination.

The path of hardware entrepreneurship is not for the faint-hearted, it will be one of the hardest things you will ever embark on and I am not trying to be funny. If you don't have the mental toughness to climb Mount Everest, the endurance of a tri-athlete, the patience of a monk, the mental calmness of a surgeon when facing tons of problems all at once, business aptitude of a MBA, knowledge of human behavior like a psychologist, having the courage of a warrior when faced with fear, be as tactical as a military strategist and have an in-depth understanding of marketing and branding like a seasoned marketer and the willingness to constantly learn new skills to improve your odds. I really suggest you put this book down and never turn the page.

Good Bye and have a normal life!

For the brave ones, I applaud you for turning the page! You are the chosen ones, you have the power to change the world, turn lives around and most importantly live a fulfilling life on your own terms, be the true creator that you are meant to be and with no regret at your deathbed.

You are a very different breed of humans, residuals, hardy, persistent, tough, brave, forward thinking, ground breaking, caring and giving. It's people like you who push the world forward. You are the very reason why we have cars, airplanes, rockets, and computers. You are the world's future possibility and now, let's get to work!

You probably already have a clear idea for a product that has been stuck in your head for years that will improve the world for the better. You are thinking this is an opportunity for you to make a mark in the world and become very wealthy while at it.

Sorry to spoil your party, life of a hardware entrepreneur at every stage is extremely tough, and rarely glamorous. Only a very small percentage of entrepreneurs are ever able to make it out alive after their first product. It's extremely rare to strike it rich on your first tries. You will be facing problems like never before and you will likely be broke like never before as well. You have to learn to swim in a swarm of problems like design issues, production issues, marketing issues, funding issues, mold issues, certification issues, product finishing issues, logistics issues, customer satisfaction issues, return issues, stock issues and the list just goes on and on. So, ask yourself, do you really want to put yourself in this misery for a shot at changing the world and a slim chance for wealth and fame? It's still not too late to put the book down and just walk away.

Despite the fact that creating hardware products are extremely tough, when done right they can help a lot of people better their life and can be the perfect vehicle for building strong brands and a profitable company. Look around, the most valuable company at the moment is Apple; selling smartphones, computers and smart watches. The richest man currently is Elon Musk; selling electric cars as I am writing in 2023. Software products are faster to create and distribute, but hardware product typically builds more valuable companies and products over time. They are also a lot harder to copy by the competitions since most entrepreneurs shy away from electronic hardware.

If you still want to go ahead, ask yourself if you are willing to commit the next 10-20 years of your life to learn the skills, and know how to be a world class hardware entrepreneur until you succeed. Of course, few may find success in their first attempts, but on average, if you don't give yourself 10 - 20 years and are willing to dedicate the rest of your life learning and working in hardware. Your odds of success are stacked against you.

If you still want to continue reading, put up your right hand and promise yourself! From this day on, hardware products are ingrained into your life, you will never stop creating and learning for the rest of your life. Nothing in this world will derail you from pursuing a successful career in hardware products. You understand this will be a one way battle, it will be a lonely one, it will be painful, everyone in your family will think you are crazy and urge you to give up and get a job, but you will never look back no matter the hardship going forward will be!

If you don't have the determination mentioned above, it's better that you put the book down and stop reading as this will save you years of fruitless attempts. It is better to give up now and probably get a well-paying job instead of trying for a few years and giving up at a later stage.

This is my last warning and you will be taking full responsibility for all the misery you will be facing going forward.

If you are still reading this! Congratulations, you have made up your mind and there's no turning back from here on.

So let's define hardware since it has a wide variety of meanings. The word, hardware, in this book mostly refers to physical products with electronic components with the goal for mass production, which requires molds making, industry designs, mechanical designs, needing circuitry and software to complete the product such as a smartphone, drones, laptops, robots, smart/AI appliance, cameras, smart watches, smart home electronics, etc.

Since the cost of developing electronic hardware that requires mold making, industrial design, mechanical designs, electronic circuitry and software development is typically too expensive to be developed by an individual or even small teams due to their heavy requirements, only large companies or very wealthy individuals with massive funding have been able to successfully bring electronic hardware into the market. This means that most people have a very slim chance of becoming successful at hardware electronics.

However, there is one place in this world that may give you just the leverage you need to create world class electronic hardware just like large electronic companies and probably faster development time and more cost efficiency. This mystical place is likely halfway around the globe from where you are now and this city is called Shenzhen.

Shenzhen started out as a small fishing village in China, a river away from Hong Kong with a population of approximately 30,000 in 1978. In 1980, it was appointed by Deng Xiaoping to become the first special economic zone of China. It became the first city in China that was open to foreign trading and in just 42 short years the population grew to 17.5 million by 2022 and ranked 14 in global GPD.

Over the last 42 years, Shenzhen has become the electronic manufacturer of the world. In the process, the city has trained millions of skilled electronic workers, tens of thousands of engineers and specialized technicians making Shenzhen the mecca for developing physical electronic products with the speed and efficiencies like nowhere else in the world!

Like there is a saying, if you want to be an actor you will want to be in Hollywood, if you want to be a fashion model, you would need to be in New York, Paris, or Milan, if you want to be a software entrepreneur, you want to live in Silicon Valley. Well, let me add one more saying; if you want to be a successful hardware entrepreneur, you will want to be working in Shenzhen. This is the reason I moved to Shenzhen to pursue the development of IDOLCAM in 2017.

Chapter 1

How it all begins

My hardware career all started in my late 20s' while I was still a passionate New York fashion photographer with the dream of becoming one of the best in the industry. In my years in New York as a fashion photographer, I have worked for clients such as Coca Cola, America's Top models and my bold photography style has attracted the attention of Chanel's chief designer, Karl Lagerfeld as a potential photographer for Chanel in 2008. However, in that same year, the fashion industry was severely affected by the financial crisis, which caused most brands to reduce their marketing effort and my photography career seemed to have come to a near stop.

During the same time, my obsession with RC helicopters and passion for photography have led me to experiment with modifying RC helicopter and video camcorders to create flying cameras which I called Helicams.

Also having already completed a handful of high paying gigs flying my modified helicams for television networks like PBS, Baylor University, Halifax University, my gut feeling was telling me there was a huge market in flying cameras.

That same year, I decided to commercialize the helicams that I have been tinkering for close to a year, so photographers and videographers can have access to aerial visuals without paying tens of thousands of dollars hiring a helicopter crew. This was about 5 years before drones (multicopters) became popular. However, besides the experience of tinkering my helicam for the past year, I didn't have any knowledge in commercializing any physical products, needless to say, a flying device. But I decided to forge ahead and after a couple of months, I came up with a rough all-in-one helicam design on a pieces of paper that can transform into all 3 different styles of helicams; underslung for more stable flying and smoother aerial footage, frontal 2 axis gimbal for more nimble and speedy chasing shot like today's FPV drones and a 3 axis frontal-slung helicam, which I prefer the most ahead of the first two.

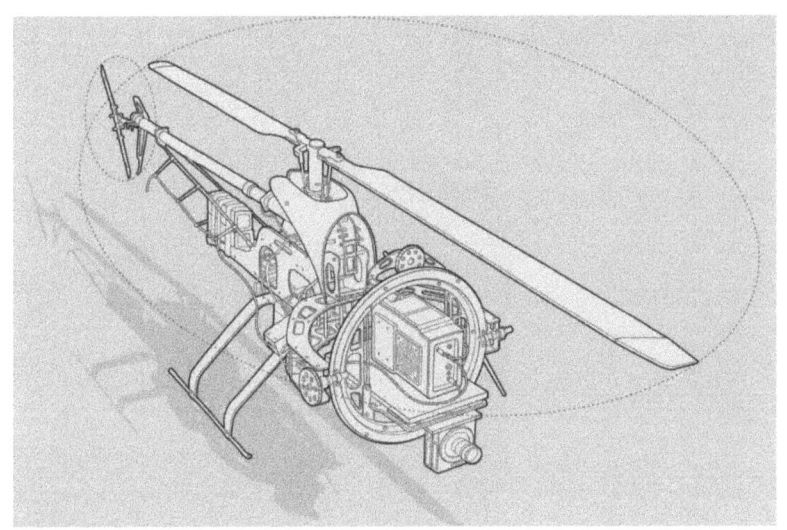

Then, I hired an engineering student, Tina Wan off Craigslist paying her $20 an hour to help me transfer my rough design into CAD drawings. After about 10 sessions of working with Tina, we finalized all the designs. I uploaded the finalized CAD to Emachineshop.com and placed 20 copies of my helicam modification kits for the Maxi Joker 800 RC helicopter.

The cost of 20 kits was around $10,000, which was a lot of money for me then and I was really nervous to get the design wrong, plus I didn't know what to expect working with an online machine shop. I was forced to make a batch of 20 units because making 1 unit would cost around $3,000. I took a chance and made 20 units, so I have a shot at recouping my investment and making some profits. The dice rolled in my favor and all the kits came out working just the way that I envisioned. My good friend, Angela Yu, helped come up with the name "Aericam" for my helicams. I decided to feature the newly developed Helicam in the New York Javits Center for the 2009 Photo Plus Expos one week before the show started. It was a rush to get everything ready, between the cost to enter the tradeshow, brochures and decoration set me back another $10,000. We had one of the smallest booths on the show, yet we probably had the most people surrounding our booth as everyone was so fascinated with the idea of a portable 6ft long 20lb flying camera at the time. Fortunately, my friend, Angela, was able to help me answer many of the sales inquiries from the tons of people around our booth. I was able to sell all 20 units for $5,000 a kit and another 8 complete build helicams for $20,000 each soon after the expo. It was a sign that I found a market need, however, being an artist that I was, I wasn't reading all these signals correctly, or making the right strategic business moves.

At this point, I decided to move back to San Francisco thinking that Silicon Valley is a much better place for entrepreneurship and also I can be back with my family in San Francisco. It was a tough decision to let go of the fashion photography dream, but I thought working on helicam may be an opportunity for me to be at the top of my industry and also be able to combine my passion for photography and tinkering into one.

My helicam designs were quite ahead of the competition, but I didn't have all the right business instinct to corner off the market by increasing production volume and marketing so I can sell at a competitive price to more people and become the leading brand in the category. Instead, I kept selling the kits for $5,000 from organic Google searches that I got for as long as I could.

Others saw I was able to sell at $5,000 for a kit, the following year, there were 2 more companies that came into the market to compete and undercut the price to around $2,000. At $2,000, there wasn't too much profit the way I was operating, it was more like a job as each kit took about 10 hours of labor and $800 dollar worth of parts to complete before it was ready to be shipped to customers.

The complete turnkey helicams took close to 3 weeks to build and tune.

My solution to the additional competition was buying two CNC machines to cut all the parts needed for the helicams in-house instead of sending the parts out to machine shops, which saved $500 and allowed me to still have a decent profit margin.

However, my biggest issue was that I didn't realize that in order for a business to grow, I need to pay for advertising and marketing to gain more customers. I was still in the artist way of doing business, if my product is good, people will come. When the demand flats out, I would just create new products like artists.

I would constantly come up with new products in my head and since I had my CNC machines plus by this time, I learned how to create my own CAD drawings. I was able to design, cut and build new products in as little as a few days. Every time, my sales would flat out, I would look to create newer and better designs to keep the interest of buyers. Looking back, since I didn't have that much competition and a very high 8% conversion rate on my website, I should have been running ads on Facebook and

Google to drive in a lot more customers. I would have definitely had a very good shot at growing the company.

A photo of an underslung gimbal mount that I made for the Align Trex 700 and 600 size helicopter with 360 degree pan capability.

Notice all this is happening in 2010, 2.5 years ahead of the release of the DJI Phantom in Jan, 2013. I was well ahead of the drone competition, but I was still clueless in how to drive my company forward. A large part was the fact that I was on a very tight budget and another part was that I just didn't know how to properly market Aericam, nor know how to find investors to support the growth of Aericam. I was also in the wrong place for creating hardware products since labor, supplies and machine shops were very expensive in San Francisco.

There's also another major issue with helicams that makes it really difficult to become a mass product like the quadcopter drones we've all come to love. Helicams are basically helicopters, and helicopters are extremely complex machines to fly, hard to maintain and very time consuming to fix after crashes. They literally have hundreds of parts that need to work perfectly in unison and it takes at least a couple of months for a beginner to get comfortable flying them. Realizing this problem, I began developing a 15lb capacity hexacopter (6 bladed drone) to replace my helicams. After about 4 months of testing, In April 2012, I released AeriCam X6 to the world. A lot of professional videographers and photographers were really intrigued by the Aericam X6 and it carries a price tag of $12,000. The build time of the hexacopter took around one week to finish, which is about ⅓ the time of our $20,000 helicams. I sold a couple of dozens of X6 without buying any advertising. Looking back, we probably could have sold at least a few hundred of them if I paid for advertising and my hardware journey could have greatly changed for the better.

Video clip below of Aericam X6 with Ken Block, Travis Pastrana for Gymkhana 5.

https://www.youtube.com/watch?v=HCDSjlAQlNc

With steady demand for my AeriCam X6, I started the first drone shop in San Francisco on Howard and 5th street. I had my two CNC machines constantly cutting parts for my different helicam kits and Hexacopter turnkey system all day long, while I was assembling kits and tuning the X6 Hexacopters for customers. A couple of months after I opened my shop, a recent Boston University grad student, Frank Sommers, stopped by my shop and hanging on the back of his backpack was a DIY FPV drone that he built himself. He was really interested in learning more about drones and had 10 months of free time till his Air Force program began, so he started working at my shop. Frank showed me the possibility of FPV drones and my goal from the very start is to eventually create a flying camera for everyone. For a long time, I realized that I needed to create a small drone for consumers in order to have a chance to realize this goal. However, the time needed to build, test, tune and package a portable drone is about the same amount of time required to build a larger drone for professionals, but the profit is 10 to 20 times less. At the time, it seemed to be impossible to pay for labor, rent and to stay in business with such a thin margin working on portable drones. Therefore, we have only experimented with a few compact drone designs, but couldn't figure out how to produce them and be profitable.

In early 2013, I began working on a handheld 3 axis gimbal for professionals with the goal of 15 lb payload. It took around 1 month to finish a working prototype with aluminum pipes and connectors that I bought from Servocity. After the proof of concept, that my pro gimbal prototype worked well, I traveled back to New York to work with my humorous German machinist friends, Wolfgang and Ruthie, who I met in Kissena Park where passionate remote control enthusiasts gathered to fly planes, helicopters and race RC cars. Wolfgang and Ruthie were both in their 60s' at the time and they were very witty and loved to crack jokes every time I saw them. They felt like 2 big kids with the ability to build anything that they wanted. Wolfgang, at the time, also had his own side project making modified RC car parts for racers, "Wolf Pack Radicals". I think Wolfgang and I connected so well because of our mutual interest in RC hobbies. I spent 2 months in New York working with Wolfgang and finished a much sexier version of my professional 3 axis gimbal, Hollywood Gimbal, then headed back for San Francisco.

Frank and I had been also testing the new Hollywood gimbal and capturing different footage to compile a promotional video for the launch. At the time, Kickstarter had gained a lot of popularity as a fundraising platform, so we thought we could launch it on Kickstarter and on our website at the same time. Since we had no prior experience with Kickstarter, we thought it was *a launch and forget situation* and the first 5 days, we didn't get any sales. We were a bit concerned, so we directed one of our customers who was interested in our Hollywood Gimbal to purchase a unit on our Kickstarter campaign and that led to more people backing our campaign. We also sent a few emails to our helicam customers about our Hollywood gimbal launched on Kickstarter and we ended the Kickstarter campaign with $41,225 selling 9 units on Kickstarter and sold another 17 units on the website during the same period. We swiftly placed an order with Wolfgang in New York to help us create the parts needed for 50 gimbals. The production version of the gimbal was much slicker than the first version showed off during the campaign.

We were able to deliver all the gimbals to Kickstarter backers and our own customers within the targeted time frame with the help from a really good friend, Brian Lok, who has a lot of experience assembling car audio systems. He was a godsend because he was able to build gimbals and X6 Hexacopter about 2X faster than Frank, or I can build them. This is our first campaign with Kickstarter, it wasn't exactly the result we hoped for, but we thought it was still a great addition to our launch effort. Afterward, we also created attachments for the Hollywood gimbal such as a 4th axis vest, 4th axis car mount, cable cam and a massive foldable X8 drone hoping to provide a complete stabilized video system for video professionals.

X8 Drone, 4th Axis Car Mount, Cable Cam

Jame Zhen, a recent aerospace engineering grad, also joined us to help design new drones and gimbals. He opened us to the possibility of 3D product designs that were more sleek looking and better fit for the consumer market that we had our eyes on. Our drones up to this point were all created with 2D design, thus our products are industrial looking, although we tried hard to add some flares to make them more attractive.

The first drone James helped us to design was the Anura pocket drone, since Frank constantly brought into the shop his FPV drone. Having had the dream of giving everyone a flying camera, I thought a drone the size and form of a smartphone would be the perfect drone for the average people wanting a flying camera.

At this point, Frank had left to pursue a career as an Air Force fighter pilot.

After a couple of weeks of working with James tweaking on the Anura drone design, we thought it was an amazing design, but we had no idea how to bring our vision to market and be profitable. We hacked the parts needed to make the Anura flying in our tests, but all the parts alone for the drone was well over $200 and the Radio and charger would be another $150, and we thought we have to sell it for $1,000 in order to have any chance of profit, but we felt the price might be too high for the mass audience. Our goal was to create a fun to fly drone to introduce to the mass market and hoping the target retail price to be around $200.

We found a drone company through Alibaba located in Shenzhen who created mini drones at the time with a lot of capabilities like auto landing, follow me and drone control via an app on smartphones and sold for around $150 retail. We bought one for testing and everything seemed to work quite well, except that the motors and power system were a bit too weak to carry our Anura design. We reached out to the manufacturer and discussed over email if they could help us upgrade the motor and power system so it could fly the heavier Anura at faster speed. They agreed to our requirement as long as we were able to meet the minimum of 500 units, plus instead of $86 for each unit it bumped up to $125 for each drone at 500 units since we wanted to upgrade the motors and power system.

We thought we might have a shot at meeting 500 minimum order quantity (MOQ) if we run a Kickstarter Campaign, knowing full well we get little traffic for Kickstarter projects unless we can drive a lot of traffic to our campaign. So for two weeks, I wrote to hundreds of journalists. Initially, a couple of journalists got back to us, CNet and Digital Trends who agreed to cover the story on Anura and announce our Kickstarter launch date and after the articles released on Cnet and Digital Trends, we quickly got a hundred of coverage from Gizmodo, CBS News, KPIX News and many other tech news websites and TV station to cover Anura.

That was a great signal that the world was really interested in our Anura pocket drone design. Since we didn't have the budget or experience to run Facebook and Google ads. We harassed every one of our Facebook friends to share the Anura drone launch and I remember for a couple of days on my Facebook feed, every other post was about our Anura drone launch.

The Kickstarter campaign was released on October 15 2014 and we decided on a 60 day campaign since this will give us more time to figure things out if the campaign didn't pan out the way we expected it. On the release day, we instantly got couple of thousand dollar worth of orders in the first 15 minutes and orders were just flowing in and we finished the first day with $34,073, the second day with $12,906, third day $6,697 and by the 30th day, we hit the $150,000 mark and we spent zero dollar on advertising. But right around this time, the company who had agreed to produce our Anura drone for us suddenly wrote us an email saying that they can't help us manufacture the Anura drones. We were shocked since our dream of creating a flying camera for the masses all of a sudden vanished in front of us. We speculated that the toy drone company noticed our Kickstarter project and wanted to make similar drones themselves instead of helping us to create Anura.

At this point, all the promised features, and price points that we had to meet got shattered into pieces. We did further research hoping to find similar manufacturers, but no luck in finding other companies that can produce similar mini drones at around $100. Since, we have never been to Shenzhen and it just seems to be too much of a risk to keep pushing on the project forward, and the cost of developing a drone from scratch and putting the Anura into production would definitely require many times the $150,000 we raised on Kickstarter. So, unwillingly, we just let the Anura campaign run a bit longer to see how much we will end up raising and canceling the project right before it ends. However, the amount of funds raised after the first 30 days came to a complete stop because during the same period, another team was running another drone campaign, Zano AI Drone on Kickstarter, their specs were impressive and they ended their project with close to $3 million dollar in funding. However, a year later, their project ran out of money and ended in bankruptcy. On December 18th, we canceled the Anura project and hoped with the data from the Kickstarter project, we can approach investors and convince them there are a lot of potentials with our Anura drones. While Anura was still hot, I called a lot of investors and got a few meetings with them. Just when I thought I had won them over to our side, the feedbacks said otherwise. They said my Anura pitch sucked. Fortunately, we got an email from LG and they were really interested in the Anura project and the following week two product managers from LG flew out to my shop in San Francisco and had a 2 day meeting with us, trying to understand the situation of our project. The meeting seemed to have gone quite well and they flew back to meet with us two more times over the stretch of 4 months with a lot of emailing back and forth discussing the spec of the project and how we can bring Anura into the market with their camera modules and sensors. We asked for $500K to develop Anura to be ready for production. However, the final decisions were not made by the two gentlemen that we have been communicating with the whole time, but by their superior who disapproved the project. At this point, everything seemed like a no go since we got no funding to push Anura forward and the design was already exposed for anyone to take. In fact, an article by the lead product designer of the DJI Mavic, Deng

Yumian now the founder of LeapX Design revealed that he did a thorough design study of our Anura on 12/16/2014. He also noted that "the Anura folding design is a very eye-catching design." Our Anura project likely prompted him to design the DJI Mavic.

You can check out Deng Yumian's article at this link, https://www.idolcam.co/mavic.html

After the Anura drone project, James also started his career as an aerospace engineer with the US Navy. Now, I have no one to help me with the 3D design. So, I started watching a lot of videos on how to use Solidworks 3D to design and after about 2 weeks, I got decent at Solidworks, at least enough to create rough designs for prototypes.

The early IDOLCAM design on the right was designed by me and the one on the left was by James in his free time.

Demo video of 3D printed IDOLCAM

https://www.youtube.com/watch?v=rSkuJFuNXx0

I was feeling pretty bummed out about the missed opportunity with the Anura Drone and thought it was impossible to create a consumer electronic hardware unless I had a few million dollars saved up, especially complex electronic products like drones and cameras. I also thought to myself that my business sense was very weak and could have played a major role as to why I didn't capitalize on the drone opportunity even though I have such a clear first mover advantage. I began studying business strategy and business models by watching all the Harvard Innovation Lab videos on YouTube and it really opened my understanding of what a real business has to be to get ahead.

After learning more about business strategies and since scaling hardware is very challenging, I began to think that hardware creation might not be my calling after all. So, I began to drift away from ever creating any more hardware and focus on creating more software. Although hardware production can be a moat only if I can figure out the production and marketing process like Apple and Tesla. On my notepad, I had written over 400 ideas over the years that could become a huge business. I selected an app idea that can connect the 1 billion car owners to move the 6 billion people without a car. I called it MasRide, an On-Demand carpooling service in February 2015. The difference between my MasRide concept and the present Uber was that the drivers don't work for the company, so they aren't confined to a certain city or neighborhood. These drivers are just regular commuters who happen to be taking trips with the same destination as people who don't own a vehicle. A modern and more efficient way of Hitch Hiking, where both the driver and the rider can be connected easily. I spent a couple of weeks thinking about the possibility of MasRide and I thought it was a great concept for moving more people more efficiently and a cleaner planet. I even created a pitching video for it. But I asked for a quote from an app development company and the price of developing a prototype for my app was $50K that I didn't have, plus my heart was still thinking about hardware where I felt I am best at.

Here is the video link to the pitch video of MasRide if you are curious. https://youtu.be/KnARYRy16OU

My itch for creating the next innovative drone was creeping back and I brushed the MasRide project aside. I also began to rethink my direction going forward and I decided to work on high volume low price consumer products vs. low volume high price professional products, since I thought that's the way I can build a huge brand and have a shot at building a Billion dollar company. My logic was simple: there is no billion dollar company for professional video products, but there are consumer camera and drone companies well over the billion dollar mark. Also at the time, DJI started selling $500 drones to consumers with the Phantom series and $6,000 drone pro version drones with their S800. So, orders for my pro helicams and X6 drones were quickly diminished. I spent the next 3 months designing and creating a new drone prototype. After completing my new drone prototype, Anura X, another challenge I faced was how to produce the drone efficiently at a price point convenient for the consumers. I was pretty clueless about mass production still, especially when the custom electronics and software required for a seamless product seem to require a huge amount of money that I didn't have. The thought of developing a complete drone from scratch may take too long to bring it into the market and probably be too costly unless I have backing of a venture.

An idea came to mind, what if I separate the project into two parts; first, an action camera with gimbal as I thought there should be a huge market needing high quality video in a compact size camera. In 2016, small compact video cameras were pretty suck in my opinion mainly due to poor video stabilization and lack of interchangeable lenses. Also, at that time, I personally had a real need for a mini video camera that can produce high quality video for creating promotional videos. I hated carrying around my 15 lb Hollywood gimbal and camera setup. It was very cumbersome to carry and also very expensive to buy pro video gears. This is how the IDOLCAM journey began.

The first working IDOLCAM concept prototype was finished in May of 2016. I started reaching out to investors for meetings to pitch them with a very rough 3D printed working IDOLCAM prototype, but investors didn't find much interest in IDOLCAM. Later I realized, Silicon Valley investors were mostly interested in software ventures since software can easily scale infinitely. Also, camera ventures like GoPro and Flip Cam have performed poorly for investors, plus smartphone cameras are slowly eating the market in the consumer camera market. My reason to keep on pushing forward to create IDOLCAM is that there weren't any consumer cameras that could produce commercial quality video at the time. So, I felt pretty good about the demand for IDOLCAM and I started to apply to accelerators such as Y combinator, Bolt and HAX hoping I might be able to land some investment this way, but I didn't get accepted by any of them.

On Jan 22, 2017, my birthday, I visited a couple of electronic prototyping companies in Silicon Valley (Santa Clara) to find out the cost of properly developing a camera for the consumer market. I remember John Park of AQS Electronics in Santa Clara gave me a rough ballpark around $4 Million dollars to develop a prototype like IDOLCAM. I was shocked and there's no way I can afford to develop IDOLCAM in the US. However, John suggested that I might want to look into Shenzhen camera companies, they may be able to help develop my camera for a lot less money.

Afterward, I asked my older cousin, Vincent Chiu, who had many years of experience working as a firmware engineer at Sony to come out for coffee so I can pick his brain on the matter at hand. He basically told me that I need at least 3 engineers (software, electronics, and firmware) to work with me for 6 months to a year to have a shot at making a camera like IDOLCAM. Hiring 3 engineers for a year sounds a lot cheaper than the $4 Million dollar, but I didn't have any idea where to find these people, nor the money to pay for them.

Couple of months later, I ran into a Russian friend, Nasim, during a hardware meetup where we gathered to show off our prototypes. Everyone came to the meeting with either a dummy mock-up of their hardware concept, or with a 3D printed prototype. But when Nasim walked into the meeting with a fine looking battery charging station that looked like the quality you would get from an electronic store, my jaw just dropped. I was really curious about how the hell his prototype looked so professional! So, we exchanged phone numbers and I asked him out for a drink at The View Lounge in San Francisco to pick his brain a few days later. In our meeting, I found out that he was in Shenzhen for a couple of years working on his prototype before visiting the Bay Area with the goal to land investments for his battery charging station for coffee shops and restaurants. He assured me that if I have around $20 to $50K depending on the complexity of my camera, I should be able to create a production ready prototype. His insight blew my mind, since the AQS quote of $4 Million had been stuck in my head of how expensive developing electronic hardware was in the US and I was thinking the whole time, I probably need a minimum of $400K to have a shot at developing a production prototype by hiring 3 engineers here in Silicon Valley. So, knowing I still have a shot if I can come up 1/100th the amount that I originally thought I needed made me feel really pumped that night. He also suggested that I visit Hong Kong and China during the electronic conventions so I can meet many factories, manufacturers and camera companies all in one spot, which I thought was a great idea. We ended our night around midnight and I was really excited about what I just learnt. Nasim got in a taxi and I walked back to my car that was parked a few blocks away.

As I was about half a block away from my car on 5th street, between Market and Mission street, a tall black male who must have been over 6ft. tall came from behind and suddenly grabbed me. My instinct was he was trying to rob me and I needed to break loose of his grip fast and I quickly turned around and swung at his jaw with my fist with all the strength that I can musk. This man was in shock after my punch, the 20 years of basketball definitely kept me nimble and in good shape. For some reason, I wasn't afraid at all, maybe it was the drinks from The View Lounge. I shouted at him, "Come on, you want more of this!" and I did the Bruce Lee stance and after about 30 seconds of confrontation he began to walk away, he probably thought I wasn't an easy target at this point. I quickly moved to my car trunk and brought out an aluminum pipe that was left over from building the Hollywood gimbals and chased after him. Once he saw me running towards him, he swiftly ran toward the alley and I chased after him and took maybe half the alley to catch up to him and I tripped one of his legs with the aluminum pipe, then he tumbled and fell on the ground. I just stared at him with the aluminum pipe pointing at his head while he was on the floor and told him "never to mess with me bro". I had no intention to harm him, but at this moment I just realized that I have the strength to rise to the occasion. I felt like I had slayed the dragon and looked fear directly in the eyes. I thought this is the turning point of my life and time for the next chapter, moving to Shenzhen.

Tip 1: If you have no advertising budget, try writing to journalists, influencers and harassing all your social media friends to share your product launch can be worth a try.

Tip 2: Don't get too excited when larger companies are interested in your project. Make sure that the person that you are dealing with is one who can make the final decisions. Otherwise, try to not waste too much of your time and efforts on helping them with their job. It's very likely that they are just there to learn about your project and nothing more.

Tip 3: Never reveal any innovative designs, or inventions to the public especially on platforms like Kickstarter and Indiegogo until you are ready for production, or better yet delivery. Because not only are you demonstrating a new design idea to your competitors, but you are also showing how profitable your design will be in the market. Any design that do well on crowdfunding platforms, you can be sure competitors will beat you to the market 9 times out of 10 because they already have all the resources that you lack. Also, it's very likely that they will create an even better and more affordable version than the one you currently have, which will obsolete your design before you are in the market. Another way to protect your invention if you are in the United States is to file a provisional patent and it is easy enough to file it by yourself by watching online tutorials if you are on a tight budget. This will reserve your right to claim the invention for 1 year and if your project turns out to be profitable, you can then follow up with a utility patent with a patent lawyer. But I much prefer to keep it in secrecy from competitors than fight in court. It should be okay to show to investors, just make sure the investors are not already invested in your competitors and don't try to ask investors to sign NDA, they will most likely just skip your interview.

Tip 4: If your idea is too big to tackle, see if it is possible to break down the project into smaller products to reduce your cost and time to market.

Tip 5: Electronic development cost in Shenzhen can be up to 100 times less in the United States, or most Western countries. Countries like Vietnam, India, and Mexico are slowly, but surely becoming the next manufacturing powerhouse and could be an option for low cost product development once their manufacturing ecosystem matures.

Tip 6: Raising angel rounds with close friends and family will have the highest chance. Do make sure they know that there is a chance that you will lose their money.

Chapter 2

The Magical City

I started researching in Shenzhen for potential camera companies that might be able to help me develop IDOLCAM. I reached out to action camera companies who are already producing their cameras with industry leading components such as Ambarella processors and Sony sensors, which was what GoPro and DJI was using at the time. I wanted to make sure IDOLCAM will be able to produce image quality meeting and even exceeding industry standards. I wrote to a few mid-size action camera companies that I thought might be a good fit to help develop IDOLCAM. I forgot the names of some of the companies that I had reached out to, since it's been 6 years already. But one of them is Firefly Action Camera, which I am still friends with the CEO, Vikin, till today. I basically wrote to him saying that I need help to develop a 4K action camera and need some modifications to the current layout and upgrade the processor and sensors to ensure the best image quality. Vikin's team wrote back said they can help with the development. As soon as I received his confirmation, I bought a plane ticket for Oct 10th 2016 headed to Hong Kong which is a 40 minute train ride from Shenzhen to check out the Hong Kong Electronic Fair (Autumn Edition) occurring on October 13-16th. I spent 3 full days covering the entire convention floor with a photography buddy, Laurance, who is living in Hong Kong. I saved every camera vendor contact that I felt had the potential to become a partner. After the convention in Hong Kong, I traveled across the border to Shenzhen and booked a room in an apartment located in the city center through AirBnB for about $20 a night. I stayed for 2 weeks and met about 6 camera companies including paying a visit to Vikin at Firefly. Some of the companies felt like they are too big to work with and won't be able to give my project much attention, some of the companies felt they are just a reseller of generic action cameras and don't have the capability to help develop IDOLCAM. So, I came up with the conclusion that Firefly may be the best company to help develop IDOLCAM, since they seem to have technical ability and are friendly to work with. After 2 weeks of meeting with all the vendors, my overall conclusion was that IDOLCAM is possible if I can come up with around $40K plus living expenses for at least 6 months. I flew back to San Francisco trying to figure out the funds needed to cover the development cost of IDOLCAM.

After I got back to San Francisco, I reached out to hundreds of angel investors, through LinkedIn and Crunchbase, but didn't have much success. Then I started chatting with close friends who are already investing in stocks, or doing businesses. A very close friend, Paul, who was investing in friends' restaurants and stocks was also interested in investing in my project, or probably just doing me a favor. Paul helped me by investing in IDOLCAM and I covered the rest of the funding with my own savings. With a bit over $40K, I headed back to Shenzhen on Feb 7 of 2017

This time, I approached the IDOLCAM project a bit differently than I did with previous projects like the Anura. I felt that I gave up on the Anura Drone project a little too early and I used to jump around between projects once I ran into problems. I made a promise to myself that this is a one way trip, I will give all I can to turn IDOLCAM into a reality. I made up my mind and promised I will not look back until I have an IDOLCAM production ready prototype in my hand. I got this strategy from the "Art of War," burn all bridges if you want to win tough victories. This concept was reinforced after I read the story of "3 feet from Gold," a story inside the "Think and Grow Rich" by Napoleon Hill of a gentleman named Darcy, who found initial success with digging up gold fragments on the land he bought, then later the gold was gone and after many days of digging, he couldn't find any more gold and sold the land and all his tools to another gentleman. The new owner found an expert in gold mining and did an analysis and told him, bedrock is only 3 feet away and that should be where the majority of the gold will be deposited. This story resembles my Anura drone venture. I found initial success with the Kickstarter Campaign, but I gave up after one manufacturer said no to me although they were a very critical part to delivering the Anura Drone to customers. I could have reached out to more Shenzhen drone manufacturers, or flew out to Shenzhen with the $150K from Kickstarter. Knowing what I knew back then, I probably made the right decision of not risking Kickstarter backer's funds, but knowing what I know today, I definitely lost a great opportunity and 3 years of my time before my next opportunity, IDOLCAM.

Once in Shenzhen, I found a shared apartment through AirBnB in the outskirts of Shenzhen, Xi Xiang. It was a 4 bedroom apartment on the 17th floor of a 32 story tall building in a gated community with 10 other similar skyscrapers. The 1 line subway station is underneath one of the buildings in the community connected to a huge mall with a lot of food and stores, so I am all covered for food and shopping in this community. My first impression of this building complex was very modern and feels like I am living in the center of downtown San Francisco even though I am in the outskirts of Shenzhen. Rent was 2600 RMB about $400 for a 12x15 feet room. I got along really well with all 3 roommates, 2 of them are recent graduates from universities in the US and came back to Shenzhen looking for opportunities and the 3rd roommate was our landlord. We often go to eat dinner together in the mall and sometimes for beers afterward. I became good friends with the Landlord, Tong Yuan, since he plays a lot of basketball and I often tag along to get some exercise. During the daytime, I would go out and meet as many camera and gimbal companies as I needed to finalize the companies to develop IDOLCAM asap. I visited Vikin of Firefly a few more times, chatting over the development of IDOLCAM, but I still have a lot of questions that were not fully answered. Each visit to Vikin, I bought snacks and fruit tea for everyone in the office. After a few visits, Vikin told me I should pay a visit to his friend's company. His friend, Sunny, is the one in charge of developing camera projects with Ambarella SOCs and Sony Processors. They are one of the few companies that specialize in developing Ambarella cameras and have the ability to customize camera projects. This is about 1 month into my second stay in Shenzhen and for the first time I realized how all the pieces of camera development come together. The type of company Sunny runs is called "Solution Company, 方案工司." In this case, Sunny and his team of 30 software and electronic engineers specializes in developing electronics and software for cameras using Ambarella SOCs. You can view them as design companies, but for electronics and software for camera products. Voila, now I understand how everyone can develop complete electronic products fast and efficiently. There are solution companies for drones, cameras, smartphones, smartwatches, and ebikes. They can customize the software and electric circuit board to meet your project needs.

However, each solution company has different fee structures and requirements. It set me back around $20K to start the IDOLCAM's camera portion with Sunny's company. According to Sunny, the $20K is just enough to cover the expense of the wage for their engineers and pay for licensing with Ambarella. The way they make money is when my product is able to sell in thousands and millions of units. They play the role of building and selling the PCB boards for IDOLCAM and in fact they will reimburse the $20K development fee once I can meet the quantity agreed on the contract. So, I thought this is a great deal, but they typically only take on projects with companies that already have a track record of selling products with high volume since if the product doesn't sell in high quantity, they won't make much profit out of the collaboration, or unless the product is innovative and that they believe to have the potential to break out in the market.

Upon meeting Sunny, he seemed to be quite friendly and I found out that their company is responsible for most of the better known action cameras out of Shenzhen and with 30 engineers working in the office, I felt very good about their technical capability. Sunny was really impressed with the rough 3D printed and working IDOLCAM prototype that I had already built back in San Francisco, but his concern was that I may run into financial issues developing and promoting IDOLCAM, as camera projects are very heavy in finance. So, I told him my plan of running a Kickstarter project after the development and a good chance of landing investment. Also I had a lot of experience with selling and manufacturing drones in the past. My bluffing made him feel a bit better at collaborating and he agreed to working together as he thought IDOLCAM was quite an innovative camera concept at the time.

With the camera development piece figured out, I moved onto figuring out the gimbal development. Sunny's company is only specialized in camera development and has never worked on a gimbal in the past.

Fortunately, a few years back, I worked with the developer of the first open source brushless gimbal project, (Simple BGC). We used their gimbal software and electronics in the past in our Hollywood Gimbals with good results. So, I figured that I can use the same software and electronics for IDOLCAM. I reached out to the owner of Simple BGC, Aleksey, for all the technical drawings (schemes) and BOM to give to Sunny's team to help customize a mini version circuit board to build the gimbal for IDOLCAM.

While Sunny's team was working on figuring out all the parts and circuit for the camera and especially the gimbal, I now had to find an Industrial design firm to create the design and aesthetics for IDOLCAM and provided the PCB board layouts so Sunny's team can start drawing the circuits and laying out all the parts on the circuit boards. It's been too long to remember which website, but I did a Google search and it was an industrial designer directory that has a lot of Shenzhen industrial design firms. I stopped by 6 different design firms for quotes and one of the design firms that I met mentioned that it is best to find a design firm with both industrial and mechanical design capability to reduce the project complexity, time and cost. I thought it made a lot of sense, so I narrowed down to 2 industrial design firms with mechanical design capability. One of the firms was less expensive at 40,000 RMB around $6,300, but the one that I was more interested in working with was "April 16th Design," because they have previously designed a smartphone gimbal that looked very posh and won a Red Dot design awards, but their asking price was 70,000RMB around $10,800, which was out of my budget.

I came back to meet with the owner of April 16th Design, Alex and told him my situation of being a solo creator with limited funds and wondering if he would be able to take on my project for 40,000RMB. After about 20 minutes of chatting, he agreed to take on my project mainly because he was interested in the IDOLCAM concept. He thought IDOLCAM was very innovative and could help them win design awards, so he agreed to work together on the project for both industrial design and mechanical designs.

Now everything needed for IDOLCAM to create the production ready prototype was all lined up. One thing I like to emphasize on is when you collaborate with a design or development company, make sure they have experience to design your product for mass production. In Shenzhen, this is typically not an issue since all industrial design firms have a lot of experience working with mold and assembling factories. But you have to be careful if you are working with smaller industrial design firms from the West, they may not have much hands-on experience with the mold making and assembly process. The last thing you want is to have a beautiful product design that is near impossible to assemble. So, any fitting and assembling issues must be solved during the design phase, or at the latest during prototype phase. Avoid making any design changes once your molds have been finalized, otherwise you will lose a lot of money, and time fixing the molds, or worse, spend even more money on remaking the molds.

Balbal of April 16th Design was assigned to work on the industrial designs of IDOLCAM and his first design iteration really impressed me. He turned my IDOLCAM from a rough concept into a world class looking product. The industrial design process for IDOLCAM went very smoothly, it took about 2 months and about 6 meetings to finalize the Project's industrial design. They also created a high-resolution 3D print of IDOLCAM that mimics what a production unit will look like. I was really happy and felt like half my dream was realized, even though at this point, IDOLCAM wasn't even functioning, it was just a realistic plastic 3D model of IDOLCAM that I can hold in my hand.

After the industrial design was finalized, I was introduced to their partner who does the mechanical design and their office was just a few blocks from my apartment in Xi Xiang. The person in charge was "Mr. Lai," also a very nice, patient, competent and friendly person to work with. His job was to figure out how to run the wires, and cables inside IDOLCAM and where the microphones, Wi-Fi antenna, screws, and battery and button locations that make the most sense for production assembly. Plus defining the dimension and shape of all 13 PCB boards inside IDOLCAM to give to Sunny's team so they can start laying out all the parts on the PCB boards to finish a working IDOLCAM. Mr. Lai's team also breaks down the 3D design into 33 tiny parts, so we can create molds to produce composite plastic parts for building IDOLCAMs. There was a feature that I wished Mr.Lai's team could help realize, which was the magnetic interchangeable lens system that I envisioned. However, they were reluctant to help me design the interchangeable lens system because they had never designed one before, nor does any other mini cameras in the market have an interchangeable lens system that they can refer to, so their logic was it is not possible, or it will be very risky for production. One thing I noticed while working with engineers, at least the ones in Shenzhen, they tend to only work on designs that they were comfortable with. In general, they don't like to take on new designs that can be risky for volume productions, which is very understandable. But my instinct is telling me that I needed an interchangeable lens system, otherwise there are no big selling points. Especially since IDOLCAM is a new brand, I need to create additional value that other compact cameras won't be able to match in order to have a chance to stand out in the market. So, I took it into my own hands and started sketching designs on the 3D program, Solidworks, to create the magnetic interchangeable lens system. It took me a couple of weeks and multiple 3D printed prototypes to finalize my interchangeable lens design. In the back of my mind, I know it's the killer feature that IDOLCAM must have in order to compete.

It took about 3 weeks for Mr. Lai's team to finish all the mechanical designs for IDOLCAM. But the final mechanical design adjustments for all the parts probably took about 30 meetings over 3 months with Mr. Lai's team to finalize.

After the PCB board dimensions were given to Sunny's team, all 13 PCB boards came back after about 6 weeks, the camera, gimbal circuits and software development ran very smoothly. While Sunny's team are sorting out bugs for the camera and user interface, I found a professional prototype making company to create parts matching the look and quality of production units. It cost around 4,000RMB, $620 to create all the plastic and aluminum parts needed to assemble 1 unit of IDOLCAM and I ordered 3 units for testing. It took around 3 weeks for all the parts to come back and I now have all the parts and electronics needed to build my first 3 IDOLCAMs. It must have taken the span of 12 hours to build the first IDOLCAM, but it was worth every minute and very exciting to see IDOLCAM slowly coming alive. I can finally relax at this moment since I didn't end up wasting a whole year of my time and Paul's money and my money on a dream, I actually have a working futuristic mini video camera in my hand.

Check out the Time-Lapse video of the first Prototype build of IDOLCAM,

https://www.youtube.com/watch?v=GOy6NhiJyJE

Tip 7: Solution Companies (方案工司) are your solution to a fast and efficient way to develop electronic products.

Tip 8: Going to electronic product conventions is a great way to meet many vendors all in one place.

Tip 9: Electronic product general workflow, 1) Defining the Problem, 2) Product planning, 3) Industrial design 4) Mechanical design 6) Electronic and Software Development 7) Mold Design 8) Packaging and Website Designs 9) Launch Strategy 10) Media Buying

Chapter 3

Kickstarter Funding

After the 3 units of IDOLCAM were finished around February 2018, I bought a ticket and headed back to San Francisco to plan on running a Kickstarter campaign to raise the money needed for production. Around $45K has been spent on developing IDOLCAM and I am pretty broke at this point. Once I landed in San Francisco, I switched into videographer mode. I went to many locations to capture as much footage as possible with IDOLCAM so I can create a great video for promoting IDOLCAM on Kickstarter. My buddy, Joe Fletcher, being a good sportsman played the main character in my video and we met up three times to shoot different user demonstration videos. Joe was the perfect demographic for IDOLCAM and very fortunate to have him helping. This is the first time that I was able to shoot high quality video with a palm size camera, it was very exciting.

Everything is now on the line, if the Kickstarter campaign comes short of $100K, it will be near impossible to push forward with the IDOLCAM project. So, with the experience from past Kickstarter projects, I did 3 things to ensure I will achieve some degrees of success with the IDOLCAM campaign. First, I did research on the most successful Kickstarter campaign in my category and it turned out to be a product named "Arsenal", an AI DSLR assistant device that raised close to $2.7 Million dollars on Kickstarter. Since I didn't have a marketing team to help, I figured it's best to model after a winning campaign and even if I can't achieve their success, I should achieve some degree of success. I also reached out to the Arsenal CEO, Ryan, and asked if they have worked with a marketing team and he shared that he worked with Jellop, one of the up and coming Kickstarter marketing firms at the time. In the past, the project owners of the Kickstarter campaigns that raised a high amount of funding typically worked with a marketing firm to leverage the marketing firm's experience and unlock additional marketing budget to achieve significantly higher funding. However, the drawback of these marketing firms typically took about 15 to 30% of the fund raised plus the amount spent on ads. So, it is a good idea if your project has a very healthy margin, or your project already has venture backing. Unfortunately, the complexity of building IDOLCAM doesn't have the highest margin when producing at low volume. I also had to offer a 20-30% discount to backers so they have incentive to pledge to my project for the Kickstarter campaigns. When I did some rough math, 20% (marketing agency) +25%(Kickstarter Discount) + 20%(Advertising Fee) + 5%(Kickstarter Fee) + 3% (PayPal Fee) , that left me only 27% of total funding for the production of IDOLCAM. Plus I still need to pay for molds, packaging, shipping, rent and living expenses. 27% funding is definitely not going to work out, so I have to forgo the idea of working with a marketing firm to give myself about 47% of the funding to pay for production of IDOLCAM. Plus I didn't want to come out of the campaign in heavy debt. The Arsenal project on the other hand is quite different. Arsenal consists only of a thin plastic box with probably just one main circuit board, the perceived value is quite high, but the cost and time required for manufacture is very low compared to a complex digital camera like IDOLCAM. Their cost of product is likely around 25% of the retail price, while IDOLCAM costs around 50% of the retail price to manufacture. We can only reduce the cost of IDOLCAM when we can reach volumes in the tens of thousands. Plus my strategy to profit is through the additional lenses and accessories that we have to offer.

Therefore, the best first product for first time electronic hardware creators is a simple box with one PCB circuit board, so it will be easy to manufacture, scale and your profit will be much higher.

The second thing that I did to ensure the success of IDOLCAM was that I needed to ensure the campaign had a lot of momentum at the very start to have a shot at creating a $100K plus campaign. In 2018, most journalists were tired of covering Kickstarter projects since they often go bust. So, when I heard back from many journalists, most of them were reluctant to cover IDOLCAM until my project was in the market.

Since, I only had 2 IDOLCAM with me in San Francisco, the 3rd one was with the industrial design firm used for a design contest. I didn't have the option to send IDOLCAM test units to influencers for review. For many large Kickstarter campaigns, creators often send their product to influencers for review to help their project get more exposure and Arsenal did just that with their project.

Fortunately, one of my good friends, Collin, whom I met while I was a photographer in New York also moved to Shenzhen and his girlfriend happens to be the famous hacker girl on YouTube, Naiomi Wu, and Sexy Cyborg. They helped me out greatly by doing a review video on IDOLCAM right before I headed back to San Francisco. Naomi launched her video just before my Kickstarter campaign and that gave IDOLCAM over 300K views on YouTube, which was a huge boost for my Kickstarter campaign.

Third, I met Vivian who works as a campaign advisor for Indiegogo, she suggested that I will need to collect at least 2,000 emails of buyers interested in IDOLCAM before I would even consider running a crowdfunding campaign. She mentioned only about 5% of the subscribers will end up pledging, so 2,000 names will only give me about 100 orders. The way crowdfunding platform works is that the initial first hour of the campaign launch is the most critical, it will determine if your project is worth it for the platform to send you more of their organic traffic, or direct traffic to other projects that are more likely to make them more money. Knowing that insight, I made sure to have a pool of people who will back IDOLCAM at the beginning of the launch. So, I also ran Facebook Reach ads for 2 months before the campaign and spent about $2,000 on Facebook ads and collected around 2,000 emails. I covered the ad fees with my credit card, it was a scary idea but I didn't have much of a choice. Until this point, I have never paid for ads, nor have any ideas of how to properly run Facebook ads, so I looked up many YouTube videos on how to run Facebook ads.

I also asked all my close friends to help me pledge to my campaign and fortunately I have 8 very good friends who were very happy to buy my camera. I stress to them to pledge at the beginning of the launch, since people love to back projects with momentum at the early stage of the campaign.

Here is my logic why I launched IDOLCAM on Kickstarter instead of on Indiegogo. Although I did really consider going with Indiegogo, at the very last minute I decided to go with a platform that I had achieved success with in the past. I can't afford to have any surprises for the IDOLCAM project. Also, Kickstarter backers are more passionate about innovative products and they are there to help advance technology and are more lenient in case the project doesn't pan out. Indiegogo is more of a pre-order platform, little room for error and you will constantly get harassed by backers if delays occur. Another reason is that after the Kickstarter campaign ended, Indiegogo can help move the IDOLCAM project to the Indiegogo platform and continue to receive orders, but you can't do that the other way around. Therefore, I ended up selecting Kickstarter for the above 3 reasons.

My IDOLCAM project launched on Kickstarter on April 9th, 2018 and this time, I selected a 30-day timeframe because with the Anura project, funding flatten out rapidly after the 30 days mark and even went negative a few thousand dollars. Since I have a limited ad budget to drive in revenue for the whole 60 days, I figure it is best to use a shorter 30-day timeframe . The week before the launch, I sent out email campaigns to notify the 2,000 plus subscribers each day and most importantly, I sent out an email just before the launch that morning to make sure the maximum number of people would check out my campaign and pledge on the launch day. The first day of the campaign, the project raised $31,270 and sold 82 units, about 4.1% of the 2,000 plus subscribers converted on the first day, very much close to the projection of 5% Vivian at Indiegogo had mentioned before. The second day $13,385, the third day $4,266, the fourth day $5,435 and the fifth day $3,907. Noticing a rapid decline in funds raised, I turned on Facebook ads on the 6th day of the Kickstarter campaign and spent close to $1,000 per day for 14 days driving in on average of $5,000 per day with around $120,000 raised when my ad budget ran out. The remaining 11 days, I was out of credit card limit, so I just let it run on its own and ended up with the final funding amount of $145,252. Looking back, I should have borrowed my friend's credit card to push the funding and pay them back afterward with a bit of interest.

The IDOLCAM Kickstarter campaign had a 9 to 1 ROI, meaning each dollar I spent on advertising, I got $9 dollar back in revenue, which was an amazing deal. I didn't realize how amazing of a deal that was at the moment, otherwise, I would have found ways to borrow more money to drive in more funding.

If you want to raise $5 million for a crowdfunding campaign, you should have a $560,000 ad budget ready. This figure matches a bike project that raised $5.5 million on Indiegogo and later got sued by its marketing agency for $524,000 of unpaid fees.

The reasons for high ROI running crowdfunding campaigns is first, when you drive in sales from outside sources, crowdfunding platforms will give you even more traffic that will lead to more sales. Looking at the data, close to half of the sales are from Kickstarter. Secondly, when the amount is rapidly rising, backers get excited and want to be part of a hot project and the first to have the newest toys.

At this point, it may seem that I had a good campaign and I was able to control my advertising fee to 11% ($16,000 Facebook Ad spent). But I got caught with another surprise, I didn't expect that about 10% of backers' pledges were not able to be charged due to credit card info errors and some changed their minds. In the end, I had about $100,000 after Facebook ads cost, Kickstarter and PayPal fees to pay for production, mold making, packaging and shipping fees. Since each IDOLCAM costs around $250 times 400 units is already $100,000, so I still need to figure out how to pay for molds, packaging, shipping and cost of living. If I can run the IDOLCAM campaign again, I would set my goal to at least $1Million with a $100K ad budget.

This way, I am able to cover all the extra costs associated with production and be profitable right after the delivery to all backers.

One last tip for crowdfunding campaigns is make sure you have a business bank account before you run your campaign since you may hit it big. Imagine you have hundreds of thousands to even millions of dollars hitting your personal account, you can be sure the IRS will come after you at a later point. So, keep all your expense receipts and revenue trackable and don't ask how I know, it won't be fun dealing with the IRS.

Tip 10: Model after successful Kickstarter projects that are in your category unless you have a professional market team to help out.

Tip 11: Your first electronic product is best to be simple to produce and hard to copy. A box with all sensors and processor on one PCB board and your unique algorithm, or technology is most ideal.

Tip 12: Make sure to have at least a couple of thousands of people signed up before launching on crowdfunding platforms.

Tip 13: You need at least a 10%-30% ad budget to achieve your funding target. For example, if you want a $1 Million campaign you will need at least a $100,000 ad budget.

Chapter 4

Pre-Order Funding

A week after the Kickstarter campaign was over, I purchased a plane ticket and headed straight back to Shenzhen to work on the production of IDOLCAM.

The first thing that I did once I landed in Shenzhen was to try and mimic the Kickstarter ROI by running Facebook ads to my website (www.IDOLCAM.co) since I am still around $40K behind on production funds. However, things didn't pan out exactly the way I envisioned, I barely got sales on my website, it was like burning money that I didn't have, a very scary feeling because I was covering the ad budget with my credit card again. I was running Facebook "traffic ads," as most Facebook ad gurus on YouTube were suggesting. However, I barely got $3,000 in sales with $3,000 spent on Facebook ads. I also tried YouTube ads, but website traffic cost twice as much as

Facebook ads and after about $2,000 of ad spent on YouTube with zero sales, I stopped advertising on YouTube. After spending around a total of $5K on ads with only around $3,000 revenue, I was discouraged and I couldn't figure out why there was such a low conversion rate on my website. I simply stopped running ads for 6 months thinking I will lose even the production funding if I continued running Pre-order campaigns to my website. Fortunately, I came across a video on YouTube, a guy named Verum mentioned running only "conversion ads" if you want to have a chance for positive ROI, all other types of ads will lose money unless you are a brand with a large budget and can wait 3 to 6 months for a return. I took his advice and instantly, I was getting 2.5X ROI. Another golden nugget I found when I came upon the interview video of Bryce Fisher for the Ravean Jacket on Kickstarter. He mentioned they wasted $5K advertising budget trying to advertise to regular consumers early in his Kickstarter campaign. He got amazing Click-Through-Rate but barely any conversions because most consumers either don't know what Kickstarter is or they simply didn't have the urge to pay for pre-orders. The moment Bryce switched to targeting Kickstarter and Indiegogo audiences, his ROI shot up like 5X. With that insight, I started running "conversion" ads targeting the Kickstarter and Indiegogo audience since IDOLCAM was still in Pre-Order mode. ROI this time shot up to 3.5X. Then I also started using influencers in my ads when I saw one of Ben Heath's videos on YouTube recommending leveraging internet influencers for a much higher ROI. I tested with Sexy cyborg and Camera Conspiracies and my ROI got up to about 4.5X for IDOLCAM Pre-orders. The 4.5X ROI is about half of what I get from Kickstarter, which is probably about right because approximately 50% of the sales are from Kickstarter and half from Facebook ads during the Kickstarter campaign. However, Facebook ROI is not constant, as soon as I scale up on ad spend trying to sell more pre-orders, the ROI would drop significantly. Also, when profitable ads run more than a few weeks, the results would also drop a bit. The next $10,000 I spent, ended up averaging 3 to 1 ROI, but my math told me that I need at least a 3.5 to 1 to not lose money. Since at the time, I didn't have any money I could afford to lose, I hit the pause button on Facebook ads again. Knowing what I know now, a real time 3 to 1 ROI ads return is actually quite good. I recently learned even professional media buyers often are getting ad returns around 2 to 1 return running regular sale campaigns not even pre-orders like IDOLCAM was at the time. But their strategy is different. They usually run both reach/traffic ads to reach a large pool of audience (Awareness Stage) that they don't expect to convert to sales at the beginning, just want to collect a huge volume of emails, so they can retarget them with email campaign over a 3 to 6 month period to convert a much larger pool of buyers for a lot less than paying for ads to Facebook, or Google. Then, they also run conversion ads to people who are ready to buy now. This method of media buying can help companies sell large volumes of products at a very healthy ROI.

This is exactly what happened, from the time I stopped Facebook advertising, I was still sending out email campaigns that I collected through Facebook ads and over about 6 months my return added up to about 10 to 1. This was when I finally realized why larger companies were willing to lose money advertising in the beginning as if they knew they will be collecting thousands to millions of emails in the process then slowly convert them into buyers through email campaigns and become profitable at a later stage. Many IDOLCAM buyers saw my ads during the Kickstarter and made the purchase almost a year later.

All the methods that I mentioned above are for your reference only, most of the methods are still working very well as I am writing in November of 2022. It may no longer work, or be less effective by the time you read my book since Facebook ads, or any ad platforms are constantly changing and the cost of running ads will increase over time. As you can see, you need to experiment a lot in order to get paid ads working in your favor, so do a lot of testing before giving up.

The past few years of working on hardware creation, I realized that creators should give a lot of thought in figuring out the demand and marketing side of things before going full speed in product creation. A lot of industry friends that I met who did well in the market all started as a seller, or marketer of a product. They are the first ones to realize the demand of the product, plus they have already figured out the channels to sell the product. So, all they need is to create a better product to complete the money generating machine.

A lot of time creators and inventors including myself have great instinct in creating new and innovative products and we innocently want to believe the old saying, "if you create it, they will come" and that is seldom the case. Oftentimes, we don't pay enough attention to all the components needed to create a complete business machine. This is what I have slowly come to realize; a strong product with poor marketing gives you at most an average business with no growth and declines quickly over time. An average product with strong marketing gives you a good business with positive growth. Strong product with strong marketing produces fast growth and that's what is needed for startups to have a shot at being the market leader. I find myself blindsighted thinking strong products may be my solution to success, but instead, it's just a requirement to even have a chance to compete in the market. Especially in a matured market like video cameras, the moment IDOLCAM is in the market, large camera companies like DJI and GoPro will put all their resources into figuring out how to level out any advantages from newcomers with both technology and marketing power to prevent any newcomers from even having a shot at competing. IDOLCAM launched on Kickstarter May 9th 2018, DJI

Osmo Pocket launched on December 15th 2018, GoPro Hyper smooth launched in September 20th 2018 even though the stabilization wasn't anywhere near gimbal level at the time, but their marketing power can bend truth slightly into their own advantage. The stabilized video advantage of IDOLCAM, which was the biggest deal in the consumer camera world at the time, yet the advantage seemingly diminished after only 6 months. What's worse, IDOLCAM wasn't even on the market yet. Fortunately, I pushed hard for interchangeable lenses, lighting and high quality audio during the development, so I still have a few angles to push the pre-order. But they are smaller advantages that are not enough to get IDOLCAM ahead unless with amazing marketing and production in place. That's why I keep saying that startups should develop in secret and come out of nowhere catching the sleeping giants off guard to have a shot. I also would add, don't try to compete for the same market with the leading brands since usually they are already seeded deep into the minds of consumers, it would be very expensive and nearly impossible to change the minds of consumers. Most new creators fail to realize that once there's a branded company in your market, it will be many times tougher and takes years to convince consumers that your product is superior and trustworthy. Generally, unless the branded leader goes bankrupt, or they really mess up big like Nokia did with smartphones, new challengers typically will not be able to overturn the market leader. For instance, GoPro spends roughly $30 Million a month on marketing, I barely had $3,000 to spend on marketing for IDOLCAM a month, so competing head on with GoPro for action sports would be a pretty bad strategy.

At the time, I marketed IDOCAM as the first consumer vlogging camera, it was an underserved and growing market which was good positioning and no large camera companies were claiming the vlogging camera market in 2018 yet.

IDOLCAM probably entered the stabilized video camera race with big camera brands by accident. The Revl Arc action camera launched their Indiegogo campaign in March of 2016 claiming to be able to achieve more stable video with the help of a single axis gimbal is probably what put GoPro into alert mode since the CEO of Revl Arc was announcing in news interviews that they were going directly after GoPro. Having over $5.5 Million venture backing from Silicon Valley investors and a very strong technical team. When the camera started shipping in early 2018, many backers were not thrilled with the performance and PC magazine gave Revel Arc a two star rating. Even though the Revl Arc had a strong team and venture backing, it came short of the GoPro 7 that had the HyperSmooth feature ready to combat their single axis gimbal action camera. Revl Arc stopped selling to consumers soon after and pivoted to capturing videos for amusement rides.

Another camera company, Revomu, a Korean company wanting to challenge the DJI Osmo+ gimbal camera. On May 27 2017, Revomu came out with Removu K1 a compact handle gimbal camera with screen built-in. The Removu K1 didn't need a smartphone to preview the images like the early DJI Osmo+ gimbal camera and was 30% smaller. This was a nice advancement that enabled them to gather some traction for a little over a year. However, on December 15th 2018 when the DJI Osmo pocket 1 came out, a gimbal camera half the size of the Removu K1 with LCD screen. Revomu K1 seemingly lost all their advantage over night and their website was taken down soon after.

The above 2 scenarios tell us that startups should not compete directly with the top branded company in your market, try to position for a market that is not directly in the path of strong competition, otherwise you will alert the giants in your industry when you are the weakest and your chance of getting put out of business will increase dramatically. Also, aim to create your product not just a little better, but many times better than the competition to have a shot at attracting growth and compete with Top brands, or at least won't get easily put out of the race. Therefore, wise hardware startups are better to create a product that is different and addresses a different need in the market to have a higher chance to succeed.

Also, the average consumer hates taking risks with unknown brands on high price electronic products, so they will almost never buy new brand products even if your product may seem to be better. You need early adopters raving about your product to create trust and influence more consumers to buy from you. Lastly, poorly made products from a new brand will almost instantly put you out of business because once early adopters start to bad mouth your product, it's over before you start. It is almost better to not come out with the product until it's ready for prime time.

However, none of the restrictions and rules applies to products in a new market. The Arsenal AI camera assistant is in a new market with no dominant players to compete with. They are the market leader from the very start and they found a market fit swiftly on Kickstarter. The Arsenal are the perfect type of 1st electronic hardware product for creators and startups. No large brand to compete with and simple to reproduce. Even though 1.6 stars out of 5 on Trust pilot doesn't seem to affect them from producing a version two of their product since there are no better alternatives in the market. Therefore, creators should try to steer clear of head on competition with large brands especially when it comes to your first electronic product. But I am not suggesting that you create mediocre products, because this won't be the right method for long term success and horrible for branding.

So, if you have an innovative product going up for pre-orders and you can get pre-sales at a profit, or close to achieving profit, make sure you spend as much market dollars as possible to generate as much funding as possible because you may only be months away from being obsolete by your market leader. This way, after all your pre orders are delivered, you will have profit to use to create a version two to put you back into the game soon after.

Also, with hardware, unlike software, you can create a minimal viable product and slowly add features to your software over time. With hardware products, they have to be precisely designed exactly the way they are intended and they don't give you the luxury to add, or fix any physical features once they are produced. So, you must perfect your design and mechanics of your product before you pull the trigger on production.

Tip 14: Target early adopters "Kickstarter, Indiegogo, Crowdfunding" for crowdfunding campaigns and Pre-Orders on websites for the best sales conversion rate.

Tip 15: Run Facebook "Conversion" ads if you want the best chance to achieve positive ROI. Run "Reach or Traffic" if you want a broad audience to be aware of your product and slowly convert them over a 3-6 month period by collecting emails.

Tip 16: Facebook Reach/Brand ads are like standing on the street passing flyers to random people who have never heard of your brand. Traffic ads are like displaying

IDOLCAM at an electronic convention where most of the people at the event probably have an interest in checking out electronics, but not in buying mode. Conversion ads are like displaying IDOLCAM at a camera store where a much higher percentage of people are looking to buy a camera.

Tip 17: Don't compete with the Market Leader, find a new positioning in the market, otherwise you will risk getting put out of the race.

Tip 18: Create the best product possible and make sure it's unique or much better than the market leader.

Tip: 19: Keep your production a secret until you have fully completed your business machine. You need an innovative product, aggressive marketing and smooth production.

Chapter 5

Production Process

With the $100K from Kickstarter, I began placing orders for lenses, batteries, protective casing, selfie stick and all parts that are confirmed for production, and all the critical components like the joystick for the gimbal, image data wire, cables, and sensors. I chose top brand components over the less expensive Chinese brand components. Although, there are also very good Chinese components, you just have to do a lot of tests to be confident. During my prototype testing, the less expensive mini joysticks made by Chinese manufacturers would often fail after a short period of use. Also, data cable connectors would easily come off upon impacts inside the camera. I figure these small savings on cheap components will eventually end up costing more money and trouble with customer returns, which is horrible for building a brand. So, one advice is really choose components carefully, they will make or break your product and brand. There are many grades of components available in Shenzhen that will be suited for different types of products and markets.

However, there are a couple of issues with IDOLCAM that have started to bother me, the 3 axis gimbal will drift off the center with extreme temperature changes. I noticed this issue when I stopped by Beijing on the transfer flight the last time I went back to San Francisco. The extreme cold temperature would cause IDOLCAM to not hold the horizon line properly and would slowly drift 5 to 10 degrees off horizon. The z axis stabilization was also bouncing up and down a lot more compared to my larger Hollywood gimbal. Initially, I thought it could have been due to being a much lighter gimbal system. The IDOLCAM was developed using the same first gen gimbal technology as our Hollywood gimbal, which was working well except for occasional motor drift after the gimbal has been in use for 20 to 30 minutes, then the motors return to home position off-center typically 5 degrees, which was pretty acceptable for video professional at the time. However, high end gimbals in the market started adding magnetic encoders to the back of each motor to achieve absolute accurate control of gimbal motors and eliminate drifting often caused by temperature changes. Another benefit of magnetic encoders is that motors also have more torque, which provide better video stabilization. Knowing that I can give IDOLCAM even better video stabilization and the consumer users are much pickier than video professionals, the slight drift on the IDOLCAM may turn them off. The thought of spending more time developing a better gimbal for IDOLCAM creeped into my mind, but the extra time and cost required was a huge issue at the time. I had no time since I need to deliver the IDOLCAMs in about 6 months and I was already over $40K short for production, so I definitely didn't have extra funds to develop a new gimbal system for IDOLCAM. It was a really tough decision. But after witnessing what happened to the Revl Arc and Removu at the time, it was a wake-up call for me that I need to make sure that IDOLCAM is all that it claims to be. If I don't get the video stabilization right, IDOLCAM doesn't really add much value in the market and is very likely to fail soon after the release. So, I bit the bullet and decided to look for a team to help develop a new gimbal for IDOLCAM. Fortunately, Simple BGC, the company that I worked with to create the first version of the IDOLCAM gimbal also has a new magnetic encoder gimbal electronics and software and I really wanted to keep on using their system since I have come to trust it. But the problem was, at this point, all the gimbal development companies in Shenzhen that I talked with have stopped using the Simple BGC to develop consumer gimbals mainly because they are 2 to 3 times more expensive than license free gimbal systems developed in Shenzhen. However, I am not comfortable trying a new gimbal system since the risk is too great if performance and features didn't exceed the current gimbal stabilizer. I reached out to the Simple BGC owner, Aleksey and asked who helped him with developing his smartphone gimbal. Sure enough, it was a Shenzhen company that specialized in brushless motors that helped Aleskey to create his smartphone gimbal using his own software and custom electronics. This motor company had already created a few thousand units for him and I thought it would be a safe bet to work with them. Aleskey gave me their contacts and I realized I had already met these people when I came to visit the Hong Kong Electronic show a year prior. You will notice all the owners of Chinese companies that I work with, I call them "boss" and this is the way people in China tend to call any business owner, or high executive of a company.

I called them up and scheduled a meeting and took a 1.5 hour bus ride to the meeting. The first meeting went well, the owner, Boss Hu, was very friendly and even picked up the tab for lunch. I also realized his company was responsible for building a lot of the RC airplane and multicopter motors for a very popular online hobby shop, HobbyKing. In fact, the prototype of my AeriCam X6 hexacopter was using their motors for testing, but I crashed the prototype after a few flights due to the magnets in the motor came loose and locking the motors in mid-air resulting in a crash. Since that incident, I swapped the motors to German made Hacker motors for the production models and my X6 hexacopters turned into reliable flying cameras. I figured for gimbal motors, magnets flying off won't be an issue since gimbal motors spin at a much lower speed than drone motors. Boss Hu, his two engineers and I sat together over tea to discuss my project. The conclusion from his team was that my gimbal development should be uneventful as they have created similar projects in the past and they quoted me 1 month to finish my gimbal prototype and only 10,000RMB, $1,500 for development as long as I am using them to produce the motors. I thought this would be an amazing deal since the development time was ⅓ the time that I expected to take. So, I gave him a deposit of 5,000 RMB on the same day to jump on the development and I checked on him a couple of weeks later and things according to him were going smoothly. Right around the 1st month, I checked with him again and he gave me good and bad news. The mechanical design of the gimbal was finished, but they couldn't create the electronic part of the gimbal. The developers they worked with no longer developed gimbals with the Simple BGC system. The reason is that the cost of Simple BGC gimbal electronics are much more expensive, which means the volume of the product tends to be lower, so there is very little money to be made in developing a gimbal with low production volume.

Boss Hu introduced me to one of his friends, Boss Lai, who can help develop the Simple BGC gimbal for me and when we chatted, I found that he had no interest in developing gimbals anymore as he believed it was no longer profitable. It's much better to spend time on other projects instead. I asked him out on a couple of more occasions and he still held a similar attitude toward gimbals and he even tried to talk me out of making gimbal products. So, I figured it would be really hard to create a product when the developer had no interest in the project. So, I started looking into the possibility of developing the gimbal using gimbal systems developed in Shenzhen. I visited several smartphone gimbal companies and bought a smartphone gimbal unit from each of the gimbal companies to use for tests. One of the smaller gimbal companies run by Boss Huang actually had the most stable smartphone gimbal in my tests, so I wanted to work with them on developing the gimbal for IDOLCAM. I told them all the features and requirements that I needed for IDOLCAM. Initially, he wasn't 100% sure if he would be able to take on my project as he needed to consult his engineering team. He got back to me a day later and told me they can develop my gimbal in 90 days. Running out of options, I thought this is the only way out of the situation and 90 days is doable, but my fear was from past experience, 90 day projects typically take 180 days to complete. I would visit Boss Huang's team weekly to check up on the progress. Right around the 3 month period, the gimbal electronics finally came together. Initially, I thought this was a great relief, I can at last move into the production stage. When the gimbal and the camera came together, I found that both the tilt and roll axis weren't very stable, even less stable than the first gimbal that I developed using the 1 gen version of Simple BCG. My fear of using an unknown gimbal system is coming true. We struggled and tried to tune the gimbal the best we could, but the video results are not satisfactory. After about two more weeks of tuning the gimbal, they finally handed the project over to another colleague of Boss Huang, who had his own gimbal system. I was like, thank God I had another lifeline. Over the period of a month, his colleague created the 3rd gimbal prototype for IDOLCAM. I had high hopes and prayed for the gimbal to work this time. After a few days of testing, the results were slightly better than the previous gimbal from Boss Huang, but still not exceeding the performance of the first gimbal using the first gen Simple BGC system. I thought the stability could be better and asked him to tune it better, but after about a week of tuning, the result is still inferior to my first gimbal. I was devastated. I was only a month away from the intended delivery date of IDOLCAM for Kickstarter backers. So, I went back to Boss Hu and desperately asked if he knew anyone else who could modify the PCB circuits for the magnet encoder gimbal from Simple BGC, I can't take any more risk of using gimbal systems that are not proven. He told me he knew another person, but they don't have a good relationship with him anymore and he gave me his phone number to reach him.

I called Boss Yang, a deep voice picked up the phone. The sound of his voice made me think he was in his fifties. After we spoke on the phone, I went over to his office the same day due to my desperation. Turns out he was in his early 30s, tall, good looking and didn't fit the image of a Chinese electronic engineer. His office had a few large silver metal buckets that were roasting Duck Shit Fragrance tea leaves and he poured me some tea and we chatted about the issues that I was facing. He calmly agreed to take on my project for just mere 5,000 RMB, 800 USD for his labor to modify the drawing of the Simple BGC circuit boards to fit my gimbal. It must have taken 2 months to have the first set of gimbal boards to be ready to test. Once the gimbal was installed with the new circuit boards from Boss Yang, it was perfect, stabilization was dead on with zero motor drifting. It was the best feeling that I had felt for a while. There were a few minor issues and he created another prototype electronic circuit in about 3 weeks to iron out all the issues before moving onto production. After a total of

5 gimbal prototypes, IDOLCAM is finally ready to move onto the next stage of production.

At this point, I told Boss Hu to begin production for all the CNC aluminum parts needed for assembling motors to build the first batch of 500 gimbals. I have also simultaneously worked with an injection mold company to create all the composite plastic parts needed to build the IDOLCAM body. It took 5 molds to fit all 32 composite parts needed to build IDOLCAM. The 5 molds cost a total of 120,000RMB close to $18,000. The mold creation process was mostly uneventful. The son-in law of the mold company owner, Mr. Zhang, was very helpful throughout the process. The creation of the molds took around 2 months and the tweaking of the molds was about 2 weeks for each iteration and it took a total of 4 months before all the molds were finalized for production.

One of the suggestions when moving into mold making is to make sure you have absolutely confirmed all your part designs with your mechanical designers that there will be no further changes after this point. You also want to test assemble at least half dozen prototypes to make sure there are no assembly issues. If there are design changes needed to make after the molds are created, it will likely affect the cosmetic finish of the parts that require changes and if the design changes are too great, you might have to trash the mold completely and start from scratch, which will lead you to lose another couple of months on creating new molds plus tens of thousands of dollars. So be extra careful moving into mold making. For IDOLCAM, I found that I needed to add 6 mini holes on top of the camera after all the molds are finalized, so IDOLCAM can record better audio. Also, I have to design an additional small part to create the wind shield needed for the internal camera microphone. Fortunately, Mr. Zhang's team were able to make the additional modification, but it also set me back another couple thousands of dollars and a month, plus there was a slight imperfection near the 5 small holes if you look at them closely.

You should also plan the injection point of each part in the most discreet location of each part with your mechanical designer to achieve the best cosmetic result. Because the injection point of each part may leave a slight mark that will not be ideal for areas needed to have good cosmetic finishes. Then, you want to select the best texture finish for all the mold parts. Instead of a completely smooth finish that can get easily scratched, you may want your molded parts to have a grained texture finish that fits your product aesthetics, so you can minimize part defects and scratches. You can also add a layer of cosmetic paint of any color and a UV hardened finish, or even a soft robbery finish to further prevent cosmetic imperfections. Then you move onto selecting the materials for your parts. ABS being the standard material used in most products, but they are softer and easier to break, so for IDOLCAM, we selected a combination of ABS and polycarbonate to increase the hardness and scratch resistance. There are also fiber, aluminum and magnesium materials for molded parts, however, they will require different types of mold and an additional process to finish the parts.

All the IDOLCAM PCBs, gimbal PCBs, composite injection parts, all finished on time. The CNC parts for building the motors had a 2 week delay, but everything seems to have gone as planned. When the news of the CNC motor parts came into Boss Hu's new office which was only a few blocks from where I live. I ran over to his office with excitement and when I arrived, I noticed huge stacks of black anodized aluminum parts placed in stacks of clear mold containers on the long working tables. I checked all the parts and everything seemed to be good at a glance.

The owner of the CNC shop that created my motor parts was there as well and it was already evening and he suggested that we all grab dinner together.

The next day, Boss Hu's engineers were examining the CNC parts more carefully and test assembled a few motors. Upon close examination, they found out that some of the holes for fitting the tilt and roll axis motor shaft were slightly out of alignment causing the motors to bind. I was very disappointed as if we recreated all the parts it would probably take another 6 weeks plus another $25,000USD

I later found out what went wrong. Boss Hu's team was in charge of hiring the CNC machine shop to produce the CNC motor parts to build the motors for my gimbal. During the prototype stage, we have already confirmed the workmanship of the motor components from a machine shop he selected. However, during the production, his internal buyer sent the order to one of his friends who runs a machine shop, instead of the machine shop that created the prototype. It's an untold rule that buyers in China often get an average 8% cut of the order from the manufacturers. Because his friend's machine shop was using older CNC machines, so the precision was not as good as the initial machine shop that made the prototype. Plus, they rushed and didn't make a prototype before moving into production. That was why we ended up with a pile of scrap metal instead. In 2019, DJI also announced that they lost $150 million to employees inflating the cost of products. So, this is something to watch out for if you are working with middlemen, try to deal with the end supplier directly if possible, to minimize this issue.

So, I ask Boss Hu's team to pick out all the good tilt and roll motor parts and start assembling and redoing the ones that were off aligned. They picked out 300 sets of motors to start assembling and were done in about 4 days. Then I brought the 300 sets of motors to Boss Yang's factory to begin the assembly of the gimbals, but upon further examination, I noticed that some of the motors were still not aligned and some don't turn smoothly. I selected about 200 sets that passed the examination and Mr. Yang's team began to assemble the gimbals. It took about 7 days for all 200 gimbals to be assembled.

The remaining 300 sets of gimbal motors that I was expecting from Boss Hu to be produced within 2 months never materialized. They were going back and forth between the Machine shop owner who was responsible for the mishap. I was losing too much time, so I decided to have Boss Yang introduce me to a reliable machine shop that can produce high quality components. Also, I had Boss Yang produce the complete motors for IDOLCAM instead of Boss Hu. Boss Hu did later pay me back part of the fund for the 300 sets of motors about 2 years later.

I took 10 gimbals assembled by Boss Yang's team with me to Sunny's assembling team to complete the assembly of the gimbal and camera. So, I can begin tuning the lenses.

At this point, no one has designed interchangeable lenses for compact cameras like IDOLCAM before and Sunny's assembly team had no experience on how to tune the lenses properly. So, I had to test and come up with a system to make sure all IDOLCAM can produce the best images possible. On the first day, I was using an older 1080p resolution monitor from Sunny's assembly room trying to tune both the 24mm and 10mm fisheye lens for each IDOLCAM. It was very hard to tell the sharpness of the images and I couldn't even tune one IDOLCAM on the first day. Then, I swiftly purchased a 4K monitor and that enabled me to confidently tune the lenses for IDOLCAM. But the lens tuning process was still very slow, 3 to 4 hours of trying different lens combinations to get lenses to focus evenly on IDOLCAM. I couldn't figure out why at first. But knowing it would be impossible to efficiently produce IDOLCAM at the current pace, I opened the lens unit to study all the possible causations. I took a closer look and realized that the magnet lens mount on the camera is likely to be the issue. Since it was made of 2 injection mold parts and a magnet ring that were assembled by hand, therefore, each lens mount was probably assembled with different precisions. Plus, the injection molded parts can vary in thickness and flatness that may contribute to the inconsistency. Since the magnetic lens mount requires the utmost precision for lenses to tune properly on IDOLCAM. I needed to come up with a better lens mount design. I spent the next few days coming up with a 1 piece design all cut with a CNC machine to achieve the highest precision and eliminate human errors. This way, no matter who assembles the lens mount, the precision will be the same. This little design change to the magnetic lens mount was a game changer, the time it took to tune the lenses for each IDOLCAM reduced from 3-4 hours to only about 8 minutes. I was really happy with the result. The production time was reduced by about 3 hours per unit. Occasionally, some IDOLCAM units, however, can still take 30 minutes to tune the lenses, but overall this is a great improvement for the production.

Tip 20: Pick critical components carefully. Choose brand components for reliability, and use affordable components if you want to build a low price product.

Tip 21: Stay away from unproven methods and systems on your first products, even if you think it will be less expensive to produce. It's better to build a solid product at the beginning. Then optimize on cost saving later.

Tip 22: Make sure all the parts are finalized with your mechanical engineer and tested product assembly before moving into Injection Mold.

Tip 23: Close check with the machine shop throughout your CNC component making. If things go wrong here, it will cost a lot of money and time to redo. "Keep a close eye on any task that you must do-it-right the first time."

Tip 24: Deal with suppliers directly when possible. The more you go through the middlemen, the higher the cost of your BOM and less control of quality.

Tip 25: Simplify complicated components, usually there are easier and cheap ways to make them if you study carefully.

Chapter 6

Cash flow, Key to Survival

About a month later, IDOLCAMs were slowly coming off the assembly line and I started packaging them to ship to Kickstarter backers.

Right around this time, funding from Kickstarter is fully depleted. Fortunately, I was still getting occasional pre-orders coming on my website to supplement some of the expenses. My biggest hope at the time was Yamaha Japan reached out and they were very interested in IDOLCAM. We have been chatting for close to 6 months on collaborating together. They were interested in placing an order for 3,000 units to sell during the Japan Olympics, plus they have a lot of audio video equipment, but lack a video camera to complete their product line up. It was a $1 Million order and we were only weeks away from signing the contract since the Japan Olympics was coming up in about 6 months. If this deal goes through, I would be able to pay off all the debts for the production plus I will be able to walk away with a few hundred thousands of dollars after the delivery of all 3,000 units. So, I was really happy that everything suddenly turned in my favor. Just like a lot of successful people say in motivational videos, success comes at the most unexpected time and the thought of a small success was just beautiful music to my ears.

Then 2020, the Chinese New Year came around and everyone stopped all they were doing and headed back home to celebrate for a month. I headed to Chongqing for a small trip to capture videos for promoting IDOLCAM. Then all of a sudden the news of a virus outbreak occurred in Wuhan. Initially, I didn't pay much attention, as it didn't seem to affect where I was at. But the seriousness of Covid-19 was growing worse by the day, so I decided to fly back to Shenzhen just 4 days into my 2 week trip. My instinct was that it's better to be safe than get caught up with a flood of people returning from Chinese New Year that will increase my odds of getting infected. So, I spent the Chinese New Year holiday packaging IDOLCAMs to ship to the Kickstarter backers. One thing that shocked me was that the shipping cost had almost doubled when the pandemic began. It started at 200RMB (32USD) for shipping each IDOLCAM to later 350 (54USD). The extra cost of shipping adds even more burden to my operation.

I was really anxious to work on the Yamaha project and really desperate to make some money fast. Initially, the people from Yamaha reached out and wished me safe. A couple of weeks later, I got news from Yamaha that Covid-19 was rapidly expanding in Japan and their office will be closed until the virus is under control. A few weeks later, I got news from Yamaha again and their company was expecting rough times ahead and the Olympics will also be canceled for 2020, so they decided to drop the order of IDOLCAM. I understood their position, as most companies were playing safe during the pandemic, their top priority was to survive the pandemic. I had the feeling the order from Yamaha was likely to be dropped when Covid-19 was getting serious in Japan. Even though I was ready for the worst, yet when I got the news, it was still very devastating to hear because my hope of making a few hundred thousand just vanished into thin air. I barely had enough money to send out units to the first 1 hundred backers. So now, I have to figure out how to pay for a lot of the expenses needed to fulfill all the backers and pay for my living expenses.

I thought of heading back to Silicon Valley for 3 months to join the Launch accelerator run by Jason Calacanis. I met Jason at the Launch about 10 months ago and someone from his team reached out to see if I would like to join their accelerator. It would be a great opportunity to learn more about startups at the Launch and meet investors while I am in the Bay Area. However, right around this time, the China's border was closed. Once I leave, I risk not being able to return to Shenzhen to work on the production of IDOLCAM.

I remembered reading somewhere in the past that manufacturers and suppliers can also be a source for product owners to get loans. They are often the easiest and fastest way to get a loan for product owners compared to going through traditional investors. So, I wrote to the owner of AQS where I first got a rough quote of $4 Million to develop IDOLCAM when I was in Silicon Valley. AQS happens to also have an office and manufacturing facility in Shenzhen. Right around that time, there were a couple of positive video reviews of IDOLCAM on YouTube by Camera Conspiracies and Ben Sin, so I shared the videos with the owner of AQS, John. He was impressed with IDOLCAM and introduced his investment partner, John K, to explore collaboration possibilities. After a few chats with John K, they agreed to give me a loan of $100,000, but they need to first evaluate all the electronic circuits for IDOLCAM to find out the true cost for the IDOLCAM production. My initial thought was to hand over the assembly and packaging of IDOLCAM production to AQS. But they were interested in the complete production of IDOLCAM. Since Sunny and Boss Yang both helped to develop the electronics for IDOLCAM for a minimal cost upfront and their business model is hoping IDOLCAM will sell well so they can earn money by selling the PCBs boards for IDOLCAM for ongoing profit and since this is the very beginning of our collaboration with Sunny and Boss Yang and they haven't recuperated enough funds to worth all the work they have put into developing IDOLCAM, they were reluctant to hand over all the production files until IDOLCAM sold the minimum of 10,000 units as stated on our contract. I explained to them that the files were just for evaluations, so AQS can work on improving the production efficiency and that once I get the $100,000 loan from AQS, I can speed up the marketing and production, so everyone will win. However, both Sunny and Boss Yang weren't convinced and not thrilled to have a third party that may come in and replace their position in the project. The negotiation dragged on for about a week and the AQS investor, John K, wasn't happy that I didn't swiftly hand over to them the production files and terminated the collaboration. I thought God closed one door and another door will be opened, but I got both doors slammed in my face and I hit another dead end.

Fortunately, Boss Yang, knowing my situation, offered to loan me around $30,000, $10,000 for his gimbal PCB boards and another $20,000 for paying the remaining payment for camera PCBs and for the new CNC motor parts. Although I would much prefer to get the $100,000 loan from AQS, the loan from Boss Yang was still a God sent because it really helped me greatly and enabled my production to go on for a bit longer.

With 300 more units paid with Boss Yang's loan, my strategy had to change in order to keep the operation going and continue to send IDOLCAM to backers. Instead of sending all the 300 units to backers at once, which will instantly put me in debt with nothing left to pay Boss Yang back his loan and no funds to continue the production. I decided to send 25% of the units to backers, 25% for paying back Boss Yang, 25% for covering expenses and 25% for future production. This was a great plan but it was missing one element, velocity. The only way this plan could work is if there is high sales volume in a short period of time, so the turnover is faster than expenses. However, I didn't have a budget to pay for ads to drive in sales and what's worse, my Facebook ad account got completely locked out for no apparent reason. Since Facebook is the only advertising platform I had figured how to get a positive ROI and with no budget to test on other platforms, I had nowhere to turn. All that I was left with was pushing marketing via all the free social media channels like YouTube, LinkedIn, Facebook, TikTok, Twitter, Instagram and my email subscriber list. I also had distributors in the US, Amsterdam, India and Hong Kong. However, without an advertising budget to let people become aware of the IDOLCAM brand, distributors won't generate too much sales. My email list turned out to be the best of all these channels at generating sales. But since I hadn't been able to grow my email list with pay ads, the sales from my email list were drying up quickly.

My plan worked the way I envisioned, I was able to pay Boss Yang back his loan, and sent more IDOLCAMs to the backers and did 3 smaller production runs afterward. However, I am still falling short of fulfilling my promise to many of my beloved Kickstarter backers who helped realize the IDOLCAM dream. Ultimately, without an advertising budget to push marketing to generate revenue at a fast pace, the daily expenses for keeping IDOLCAM in production were eating up a good part of the profit. Plus, my Facebook ad account was locked and since I was in Shenzhen during the pandemic, I couldn't meet Silicon Valley investors in person.

If I had to develop IDOLCAM all over again, I would still take the same route to develop in Shenzhen. The only thing I might change is probably head back to Silicon Valley right around the time when I didn't get the funding from AQS to focus on fundraising because the $20,000 from Boss Yang was just too tight and I can't make any meaningful business moves with such a tight budget. I was buying time and hoping the economy would turn better.

One more thing I would change is I would start with a product that has a production cost under $50 if possible. This would be 5X less pressure than the current production cost of IDOLCAM's $250 per unit. For instance, most Shenzhen manufacturers won't produce products under 500 units and typically they expect a minimum of 1,000 units. In order for manufacturers to bring the cost down and at the same time make some money on the production, there must be a minimum of 500 to 1,000 to be mutually beneficial. That means I would need a minimum $125,000 for 500 units and $250,000 for 1,000 units. That's a lot of money for the average creators and startups. But if I have a $50 product, 500 units would be $25,000 and $50,000 for 1,000 units, which is a lot more manageable and 5X less risky.

In all, this is definitely not the end of IDOLCAM. In fact, this is really just a start for IDOLCAM. As I mentioned at the beginning of this book, I will spend the rest of my life in hardware products and I am not in a rush to achieve success. Stars will align eventually and when it does, I will be ready for it. Also, I have been planning for a version 2 of IDOLCAM and right now I am probably in Silicon Valley chatting up with like-minded investors on how to dominate the consumer video camera market.

When I started my hardware journey, I didn't find the info needed to minimize the mistakes that I had made when developing IDOLCAM. I hope my mishaps and the tips that I gathered along the way can serve as a guide and reference for hardware entrepreneurs and creators to navigate around obstacles and successfully build the next billion dollar hardware brands.

Chapter 7

OEM & ODM

IDOLCAM is a custom build product with the goal to address issues that have been overlooked in the consumer camera markets. The Magnetic Interchangeable lens system, 3 axis gimbal, interchangeable lenses, and flip screen were pretty foreign to many camera solution companies at the time. Even till this day, no other camera company came up with a true interchangeable lens system for compact video cameras. Custom design products are exciting for early adopters and perfect for companies that have a large marketing budget and are able to send tons of sample products to all top influencers to educate the market. It's a great strategy to overtake a specific market like when Apple took over the smartphone market with Iphones. The most expensive cost of any innovative product is the cost to educate the market of the advantages of your innovative product, otherwise the average consumer will not understand the advantages and will just pick a product that they understand and believe to be their solution.

Innovative products are very risky first products for first time hardware creators to attempt since there are a lot of unknown elements but the flip side of the coin is that it can award you awesomely if you can realize a flawless innovative product and have the marketing and production ready to support the growth. This typically means startups with venture backing. However, most first time hardware creators are in the stage where they are the most lacking in funds, which may be more beneficial and faster to try the OEM or ODM route. It's also much less hands on and you don't need to be in Shenzhen throughout the development phase if you find a trustworthy OEM, or ODM company.

OEM companies are electronic development and production companies. They typically specialize in popular electronic product categories, such as laptops, action cameras, smartphones, tables, smart watches, ebikes, etc. They usually already own and sell products in the category and have a design team, prototyping, certification, production, packaging and logistics capability. Oftentimes, they are already a good size company that can support product development in all stages. For example, if you to go to a laptop OEM company and you select a laptop that had already been selling, but instead of plastic casing, low resolution webcam, cheap speakers, low resolution monitors and boring keyboards, you can ask the laptop OEM company to make the casing in red anodized aluminum, high resolution webcam, high-end loudspeakers, 120hz gaming monitor, backlit keyboard and even a more powerful processor. Any changes that are relating to upgrading or downgrading the specs of electronic modules, the material used and design of the casing are usually well within the capability of OEM companies. The development cost will be lower than if you created the same product from scratch. Surprises are usually well under control and the production process will be better managed. When dealing with the OEM product development, pay attention to how the product ownership is defined. Typically, most of the intellectual properties belong to the OEM companies unless you bring in features that have been patented by yourself. You want to add to the contract that "no other companies can use the same color scheme and unique designs that have been co-developed. So, you can at least have some degree of uniqueness when your product is selling in the market. However, with OEM products, you are still customizing a product, so creators need to be able to come up with funding needed to produce a minimum of 500 to 1000 units and marketing and logistics in place to keep the business wheel spinning.

The GoPro started as an OEM product. According to the article on pevly.com, the founder of GoPro found the right OEM camera company while browsing camera trade shows for 2 years. He only exchanged emails and a phone call with the Shenzhen camera OEM Company and eventually wired $5,000 to create the mold which later became the first GoPro camera, a 35mm waterproof still photo camera. With the success of the 35mm camera and a $235,000 family loan, which enabled GoPro to create more camera iterations that later turned into the billion dollar camera company that we all know today.

An even more affordable, easier and faster method to create hardware products is through ODM factories. Instead of making custom product changes to differentiate your product on the market, you simply select an ODM company in the product category that you are interested in. All you need is ask the ODM Company to change the brand name and logos on the product and packaging. The advantage of working with ODM is that you can start selling in the market in a matter of weeks instead of months with OEM product developments. You don't need to worry about production issues and the minimum order volume can be as low as 10 units. A good strategy working with ODM product companies is to select products that are new and in a growing trend with no clear brand leaders in the market. All you need is to focus on marketing and logistics to do well and start generating profit as soon as you sell your first unit. Some good ODM product examples are electric bikes, electric scooters, bluetooth headphones, bluetooth speakers, and more.

One thing you want to make sure when working with an ODM company is that they can keep up with production in case your sales volume increases. The biggest concern working with ODM is probably quality control, which you can test by buying a few of their products on different days to check on their quality consistency. The other concern is logistic speeds, since they are coming from overseas, the shipping time may be too long unless you pay a lot for DHL, FedEx and UPS. Once you double check on the product quality, you can order a minimum quantity to make sure you have enough stocks that you can provide fast shipping to your customers in your home country. This way allows you to check each product before sending it off to your customers which can help get better user ratings and less returns.

If you want to find the lowest cost OEM and ODM companies, instead of looking on AliExpress.com or Alibaba.com, which are designed to serve western customers, you can also try www.1688.com which is the Alibaba.com for China and you can usually find better prices there. You can also check out Taobao.com, the Chinese version of Amazon. You will be amazed that there are a lot of innovative gadgets that you may not have seen before. Also, many products are roughly 1/4th the price you will find in the western world. You may have to get help from a Chinese speaking person, or use tools like Google translate to communicate with these factories/companies. You may need VPN to get these websites working properly, but it is worth the effort.

Chapter 8

Growth Marketing

With all these years of experience in hardware products, I believe one of the most important skills for creators and entrepreneurs to have in order to achieve success is to master marketing. Most creators, however, have too much pride in their creations and often think a good product is enough to create success on its own. Yes, one of the best hardware creators, Elon Musk, stressed that his product is king and he told the media that he doesn't advertise his Tesla electric cars. But don't forget, Elon musk already had $176 million when he started Space X and had invested $6 million into the early electric car company, Tesla. He also has over 117 million Twitter followers, which means every one of his tweets is worth millions of dollars in advertising. So, if you don't have a massive following, or wealth like Elon, you, or someone in your team must master marketing in order to be seen in the market. Because with great marketing, you will have good sales volume and revenue that gives you the flexibility to hire talents you need to reach the next milestone.

Another hardware giant, Apple, you would think they are the best technology company with constant innovation. But there is one more factor that really separates Apple from hardware companies like Dell, Lenovo and that is the fact that they have the best marketing and branding among all tech hardware companies. The prestige branding allows Apple to charge more money for their products and results in more money to invest into the product development, branding and marketing that give them the lead year after year.

My Anura pocket drone was able to raise $150,000 with zero advertising fund, while my IDOLCAM required $16,000 Facebook ads to achieve the $145,000 on Kickstarter. The difference between the two products is "novelty", the Anura drone was able to get a lot of free press because at the time, drones were a very hot product category. IDOLCAM, on the other hand, is in the camera category which is a legacy product category that was not as newsworthy. The number one attraction for consumers is novelty, since everyone wants to be the first to experience the newest and coolest gadget and have bragging rights in front of friends and families. Therefore, if you want a lot of free attention for your product, you need an innovative product in a new category. Electric cars are a novel product in a new category during the early 2010 and Tesla is enjoying a lot of free press, sales and investments. If your next product is in robotics, flying vehicles, VR goggles, hydrogen cars, quantum computers, then you can get a lot more press coverage than products in the cameras, tablets, laptops, and smartphones category.

Therefore, in order to have a shot at creating a successful product as a resource lacking startup, you need an amazing new idea that will stop anyone in their path, but the product needs to be easy enough to produce and you will need strong marketing tactics to knock it out of the park.

The first marketing step for any creator is to create an ecommerce website once you have decided to create or start selling a new product soon. A website can help you with 3 critical tasks. First task, which is an absolute must, you need to figure out the best way to gather website visitor emails. Depending on your product, you can try free product giveaways, product discounts, free tips, free tutorials, etc. to entice visitors to share their email with you. This way when your product is ready to launch, you already have a target audience that you can market to. The best thing about email lists is that you can reach out to your subscribers without needing to pay every time like pay ads. You can also look into an email dripping service that can help you send automated emails at set intervals to get new subscribers educated about your product's different advantages over the competition, so they will be more likely to buy from you than your competitor. There is a marketing rule of 7. Meaning, you need at least 7 touch points for consumers to understand and trust your product in order to take action especially if your product carries a hefty price tag. Email campaigns are the most economical method to stay on top of the mind of your potential buyers, so focus hard on getting more emails. Email campaigns also are the highest ROI marketing activity with an average of $36 return on every $1 you spend according to statistics from Constant Contact.

Second task is to set up your website for pre-order even when your product is not ready yet. Pre-order is a great way to gauge the desire of your product in the market. If you can't get anyone to pre-order on your website, then there is usually something wrong with either your product, or the way you set up your website. Pre-order is also a great opportunity for you to optimize your website conversion rate. If you are able to get some pre-orders for your product, then it should be able to sell well once you have products in stock. Also, pre-order will give you a much better idea on how many units of your product you will need to stock for your launch. Tesla, Apple and many large brands use pre-orders to generate revenue before the products are even available and it's a great way to gauge demand. Tesla got over 1.5 million pre-orders reservation for Cybertruck over the past 2 years with $98 million in revenue without delivering a single car yet at the time I am writing.

Third task is that your website can help start conversations with influencers and journalists that would be interested in covering your product launch. You want to build a list of influencers and journalists that can help you educate the market about the advantages of your product. They can create content on your product that you can leverage on your website and in pay advertising. They will serve as the best form of social proof that will help visitors who have never heard of your brand before and still be comfortable enough to risk their hard earned money to buy your product.

Here is a general guideline for the first ecommerce website for new brands wanting to convert visitors into sales on the website. This is my own personal experience and distillation of hundreds of articles and videos that I read and watched on website optimization.

1. Define your core audience. IDOLCAM's core audience are content creators and GoPro's are athletes. You want to know the problems that they are facing, people they aspire to become, and the dreams or goals they have.

2. Create a shocking headline that talks about the current problem that your core audience might be facing and how your solution will help them turn into the person they are aspiring to become and as a result they will reach their goal or dream. For example, Aptera, a solar powered car brand, "The last time you ever pay at the pump, pioneering a cleaner world for the next generation." The headline will be the first item your website will load, so make sure it's a point that glues your audience from clicking away.

3. You need an extremely beautiful and mesmerizing landing image to stop the attention of your target audience

from clicking away. You may want to pay a photo pro to shoot and photoshop this image because it's the most critical item on your website as it sets the tone of your product and brand positioning. You can also try AI image generating programs such as DALL·E 2 and Midjourney may also work.

4. Call-to-Action overlaying on your landing image. It can be "Buy Now" "Pre-Order" "Subscribe," and state your goal of action here, so the visitors are aware of what they should do on your website. For best results, only use one call-to-action throughout your website for the highest conversion rate.

5. Phone number should be on top of the website, or somewhere easy to find to signal potential buyers that you can be reached when they need help. Especially with older buyers demographic, many won't buy from companies that don't have a contact phone number.

6. Any media mentions, renowned clients, reviews from industry figures and review rating should be just below the landing page image. This will signal to potential buyers that your product has been tested and they are not a guinea pig.

7. Five point highlights, advantages that your product has over the competition. This is used for all Amazon products to quickly help customers to understand the advantages of your product at a glance.

8. An explanation/promotional video that explains to potential buyers the who, what, why, and how of your product. Our IDOLCAM promotional videos are all shot with IDOLCAM. If you want to shoot your own promotional video, IDOLCAM would be a very good choice. Or you can hire video professionals to help if you are not comfortable making your own promotional video.

9. Call-to-action below the video should be the same call-to-action as the one on the landing image. You want to use the same call-to-action throughout your website for the best results. Avoid having many different call-to-actions.

10. A story why you have created your product. Walk your core audience through the problems of past products that you have tried with poor results. And why your solution is better than other products on the market. For branded products, they don't need to persuade the buyers, but as a new brand on the block, you have to answer every possible

objection from buyers to increase your sales conversion rate.

11. Provide all the benefits of your product below your story. Use copywriting, images and video to explain the benefits and also address any hesitations and questions that your potential buyers may have.

12. Awards your product has received, user testimonials and influencer reviews. Video testimonials are the most persuasive, but photos and statements can also suffice.

13. Give potential buyers the ultimate offer that they can't refuse. Create a package with accessories, tutorial to make your offer look way more valuable than the price they are paying for. The offer is the single most important aspect for a high conversion rate, so you want to test different offers. High purchase frequency products such as contact lenses, food delivery, you may even test break even, or lose a little bit on the first sales and make profits on repeat sales.

14. Your website must be working on both smartphones, tablets and computers. You also want a fast browsing website to minimize bounce rate. You may want to look into CDN (content delivery network) like Cloudflare to increase your website speed and also hire a website

master to clean up your website code so as to further speed your website for the best chance of sales conversion. You can check your website performance on https://pagespeed.web.dev/

15. Look up website builder platforms like Shopify for ecommerce stores, ClickFunnels for single product websites and Weebly for easy all-in-one ecommerce website platform with email marketing, email automation and affiliate program options.

Spend as much time as you can to learn all about marketing and branding, because your hardware product won't go too far without them.

Chapter 9

Branding for Profit

Many entrepreneurs think branding is only for large companies, or building the brand only after the company grows to a large size, or generate a certain level of revenue. On the contrary, to build a strong business and to achieve the best success rate, you should be thinking about branding at the very start of your business planning. Because thinking about your branding at the early stage of your venture forces you to identify your core audience that you will be serving, their psychographics, the market segment, product positioning and your mission statement for the company. Having your core audiences' psychographics, market segments, product positioning and your mission statement nailed down will give you a much clearer perspective for marketing and designing your product, which will dramatically reduce your marketing cost and better market penetration.

For instance, if you are designing an ebike for an audience in the 20s vs. someone in their 60s, the ebike will look and perform very differently. Audiences in the 20s will probably be looking for performance, good price, design style and brand. Audiences in their 60s are probably looking for an ebike that is reliable, easy to get on and off, long endurance, the style is typically a less important factor for their purchase decision.

Imagine if your ebike is designed with average styling, average performance, average weight, average reliability and price, your ebike will neither appeal to audiences in the 20s, nor people in their 60s. What is worse, you will be competing with many established ebike makers, which to most consumers, they will never pick a new brand with average features. Also, you won't know who to target your pay ads to and your copywriting will probably not be very compelling, since you don't have a target audience and you don't have a clear identity that relates to the buyers.

Now, let's imagine your ebike is designed with a healthy, high net worth retired elderly in mind. Your design, marketing and media buying team can be much more precise in addressing the needs of this segment of high net worth elderly. Now, let's imagine your design team came up with an ebike that is a tricycle with a large capacity battery for the longest range in the class, a soft cushion seat with backrest for 2 people so their spouse, or friends can ride together. Vintage styling, large back view mirrors for safety, a horn to alert pedestrians, huge bright lights that cars on the road won't miss, front and back suspension for soft smooth rides and easy to get on and off and the option to paddle the bike to exercise their body or electric assist when they get tired. Your marketing team can now easily come up with the following brand name "The Golden eBike," brand message, "The Rolls Royce of Electric Bicycle" and marketing message "Ride to Health in Style & Comfort." Your media buying team can now precisely target Google AdWords for terms related to "Elder and luxury bikes" and Facebook ads targeting retired individuals in high income brackets and in areas such as Florida, Santa Cruz, Santa Barbara and similar locations that have a lot of sunny days with a lot of high net worth retirees.

Thinking about branding at the beginning of your venture will dramatically reduce your marketing and advertising cost and a much better conversion rate since you are not wasting advertising dollars on an audience that doesn't really care for your product. The last thing that any entrepreneur wants is to create a product that is not squarely addressing the needs of target users because your company will be many times more likely to fail without passionate users spreading your brand to their friends.

By addressing the needs and issues of your target audience better than your competitors, you will help your brand stand out in the market. Over time, with effective marketing, your brand will automatically flash in the minds of your target audience who are ready to make a purchase for the Golden Ebike, or make recommendations to friends who are looking for a bike for the elderly.

An easier way to understand branding is to treat brands like people's reputation. Ask yourself how you would want others to view your brand. Is your brand's reputation a cool, talented, nice, mean, elite, athletic, spiritual, active, smart, inspirational, happy, or a positive person etc.? As we all know, a person's reputation is developed over a long period of time, the same is true for building a company brand.

It takes a long time for your target audience to get to know your brand and takes many encounters to earn their trust. The longer your target audience knows about your brand the more loyal and more likely they will buy from you. Once you have earned the trust of your target audience, your brand will automatically become their choice whenever they are looking for products in your category.

For instance, Coca Cola spends an average of $4 billion a year to remind you of their brand and their reputation as the joyful drink to share with friends and family. Their average revenue from 2018 to 2022 is close to $40 billion which gives them a ROI ratio close to 1:10. Every $1 they spend on the Coca Cola brand generates about $10 in sales, which is an extremely healthy ROI for a commodity product. Coca Cola has dominated the consumer mind whenever you need a Cola drink. Just the Coca Cola brand alone is worth $98 billion, about 36% of Coca Cola's total market cap of $275 billion in 2022.

Branding is really the biggest competitive advantage for a company hoping for high profit, high growth and longevity. In fact, a strong brand eliminates most of your competition, so potential buyers will automatically seek your brand to purchase instead of others unheard of and untested brands. The earlier you start to build your brand the stronger the bond with your target audience will be and sooner you can enjoy the benefits of being a name brand in your category.

Chapter 10

Timing, the X Factor

Having a great product, amazing marketing and strong branding are critical elements to building a successful hardware business. However, without good timing, you may never see the day of reaching success. Entrepreneurship is like climbing Mt. Everest. Not only do you have to be in great physical shape, have a lot of financial backing, months of planning, but most importantly you need the right timing if you ever want to climb to the top of Mount Everest. May is typically the only month in the year that climbers can have a shot to reach the peak of Mount Everest since weather turns warmer and wind becomes calmer during this time of the year. If you miss this window, typically you will have to wait another year for the attempt, or you will likely risk death.

Timing for entrepreneurship is just as critical as climbing Mount Everest, the only problem is you will have little idea as to when the timing is best to begin and end. When I started IDOLCAM, it seemed to be the perfect timing as more and more people were creating video content for YouTube during 2018 and there weren't many good compact video solutions for consumers to create video for YouTube. By the time IDOLCAM was ready for the market in early 2020, Covid-19 occurred, which stopped all traveling worldwide where a good portion of our sales were coming from. We also lost a $1million contract with Yamaha due to Covid-19. Electronic video stabilization (EIS) also maturing for smaller cameras like on GoPro and Smartphones, video stabilization used to be a major problem for all video cameras; the 3 axis gimbal alone on a small camera like IDOLCAM would be a major selling point and breakthrough for the camera world at the time.

The first video stabilization solution, Steadicam, was introduced in 1975, 48 years ago, a bulky counterweight video stabilization device that revolutionized movie making and is still being used in many of today's movie sets. In 2013, 10 years ago, Freefly Systems borrowing technology from drones introduced the first commercial video camera stabilization gimbal for ground video cameras selling at $15,000 a unit. Electronic gimbals are much lighter than Steadicams and also a lot easier to operate, which got all film and video makers very excited at the time. In 2018, during the development of IDOLCAM, GoPro was the first company to come out with an effective built-in Digital Video stabilization (EIS) onto the GoPro 7 with acceptable stabilization results for consumers. Around 2 versions later with GoPro 9, the video stabilization is almost as good as a gimbal. Although there are some slight drawbacks to using EIS, since cameras using EIS are sacrificing around 20% of image quality and poor stabilization results in dim lighting, most consumers will not notice the difference.

As you can see, you can't predict the timing of starting your venture. The first video stabilization device was invented 48 years ago, the second innovation was only 10 years ago and followed 5 years ago. Unlike Mount Everest there is a pattern when you will have the best weather to climb to the top. With business ventures, you can only rely on your instincts and a lot of luck.

The founder of IDEALAB startup incubator, Bill Gross once did a Ted talk and he mentioned that he surveyed over 200 startups and he found the number one contributing factor for successful startup is timing at 43% of the time, outweighing a strong team at 32%, followed by the Idea at 28%, business model at 24% and lastly funding at only 12%. He also mentioned that the success of AirBnB is greatly contributed by its perfect timing where consumers had just been through the 2008 recession and were looking for ways to save money during their travels. If not for the lack of budget everyone was facing at the time, few would be entertained with the idea of renting rooms from strangers. The same was true for Uber. People were having trouble landing jobs right after the recession, Uber came out and provided many gigs for the unemployed, which timing played a major role to Uber's massive success.

This is why, at the beginning of this book, I mentioned that if you want to succeed at being a successful hardware entrepreneur, you need to have the mindset to be ready to stick at the creating hardware products for at least 10 to 20 years because sometime the market is just not ready for your product if the idea is too far ahead, or the demand for the product just wasn't there, or a financial crisis just occurred, a pandemic that shutdown the world like Covid-

19, a war that tore apart your country, your marketing funding is too limited to do any damage in the market and the list just goes on. So, you really need to be like the Energizer bunny, keep your operation as lean as possible and for as long as possible till you find good timing and demand for your product in the market and go all in once the environment is ripe.

Also, at the beginning of your hardware venture you are probably doing a lot of things either wrong, or not very efficient. Your financial backing is the weakest, doing everything yourself and if you are lucky you may have a small inexperienced team to help out and a small number of clients supporting your growth. All the odds are stacked against you. Thus, 1-3 years of your venture are focusing on surviving and 3-5 years to stabilize and the later years to refine and reinvent your product offers and hoping for the right timing in the market to have the chance to hit it out of the ball park.

Hardware venture is a game of patience and repetition. You have to go past the first couple of years of the learning curve to have a shot at success! So, never give up when faced with adversity and keep on innovating. There is a saying, entrepreneurship is not about making money, but about serving people with the problem you are solving. The negative effect when your product becomes an effective solution for people facing the issue is massive wealth generation.

Chapter 11

Confidence & Mental Toughness

Everyone's confidence and mental toughness level will vary greatly depending on their past experiences with winning and overcoming. With hardware entrepreneurship, confidence and mental toughness are critical traits that you will need immensely in order to tackle many tough problems that you will be facing along the way. Fortunately, these two traits can be trained through sports and games.

During middle school, my older brother would drag me to the playground to practice his baseball pitching. I would help catch his pitches and throw it back to him. At the beginning, it was a very scary experience to have a rock-like object coming at me at around 80 mph because if I didn't catch the ball, I would get a pretty bad bruise. After a week of practicing, my fear of getting hit by the ball vanished.

Slowly, I started getting interested in baseball and practiced with my friends daily after school was over. On my free time, I would also go to the library and borrow books on how to pitch curve backs, backdoor fast balls, changeups and knuckleballs. Over time and with a lot of practice, I had good command over where I wanted the pitches to land in the strike zone and managed to have a very effective backdoor fastball. During my freshman year in high school, I joined my high school baseball team. I got my first chance to pitch in an official game during the 7th inning when our team was down by 3 runs. The coach probably thought it would be a good time to test out my pitching skills since the game was likely a loss anyway. My heart was pounding faster than ever as I have never pitched a real baseball game before. I was mostly throwing a backdoor fastball with a mix of a curveball to change up the speed a bit. The first 3 batters all got stroke out, the next 6 batters were either stricken out or grounded out with zero hits given in 3 innings. After the game, the umpire came up to me and said my pitches had the most ball movement of any pitchers that he had seen, his head got a bit dizzy after watching my pitches. What the umpire told me gave me a lot of confidence as a young pitcher, plus the fact that 9 batters in a row didn't even score a hit on me made me feel really good and that my efforts didn't go to waste.

At the time, I wanted to become a baseball pro one day, however, I was 5'8" in middle school and I was still 5'8" in high school, so I started playing basketball hoping I would grow a few more inches to give me a better chance to compete baseball at a higher level. At the beginning, I was a pretty average basketball player, barely touching the bottom of the basketball board and average speed on the court. After a couple of months of playing, I started to fall in love with playing basketball. Slowly, my interest turned to basketball. Again, I borrowed books on basketball from the library and studied how to shoot the basketball and learn the game. I was playing basketball 7 days a week for an average of 5 hours a day. I also practiced a lot with a friend of my brother, Nam, who was the only Asian basketball star on our high school varsity basketball team. He was the quickest basketball player that I know in my area with a deadly accurate shot anywhere on the court and an amazing penetrating ability, perfect all around basketball player except being the same height as me at 5'8". Despite his smaller stature, his speed and accurate shot enables him to effortlessly score on players much taller than him. Since he was the best player around my area, I always called him out to practice together. As I know, playing with the best player is the fastest path to improving my basketball game. I also purposely go to gyms in the hoods to play with players who are physically and mentally very tough and constantly want to break me down with trash talk and their athletic abilities. I loved playing in these challenging environments and facing tougher players as it helped me gain more confidence and agility. This was where I learned how to reach deep into my heart and mind to stay calm and confident during tough moments. It was basketball that taught me that confidence is the single most important factor in winning the game. Days that I am confident, whatever I toss up in the air, the ball pretty much goes in 80% of the time, days that I don't feel 100% confident, maybe 30% of the time the ball will go in the rim. In basketball, people call it "In The Zone" when a basketball player makes most of the shots he tosses up. I found tricks from reading basketball books on psyching up the mind that help athletes to be "In The

Zone." Whenever I needed the extra boost of confidence and to bring out my top performance, I would repeat to myself "these players are okay, but they are garbage compared to me, I am the world's best basketball player!" and I would repeat this phrase 10 to 20 times in my mind to psych me up and help me perform my best.

Having confidence and suppressing fear from entering the mind is the key to being the best that I can be. I also got rid of the concept of "failing" through playing basketball. The more I lose to better players, the more I can analyze where I can improve my basketball game. Imagine, I am afraid of losing in the game of basketball, I would either play with players who are much worse than myself, or would never play with players who are better than myself. As a result, I would never grow my skill as a basketball player. The same applies to business, never be afraid to fail. In fact, failing is part of the business description. It is the best way to learn fast and reiterate to a better version of your product venture.

Through basketball, I also learned to bear tremendous physical and mental pain as many of our basketball practices on my high school basketball team turned into 5 hour sprint sections that pushed the limits of our body. We constantly have to force our mind to negotiate with our legs and body to keep on moving forward. My body was probably fittest at 16 to 18 years old right after all the basketball training going from barely touching the bottom of the basket backboard to grabbing the rim in about 2 years and from an average speed player to being known as "Turbo" on the Brooklyn Sunset Park playground while I was working as a fashion photographer in New York. As you can see, I have completely transformed as a basketball player in around 2 years. I learned the pattern of whenever I focus on a particular subject that I am very interested in and if I completely dedicated myself to the subject, I can usually be in the top 10 percentile.

In sport, top 10 percentile probably means that I am better than most people on the playground and able to compete at high school level. To compete at the college level, I probably need to be at least top 2% percentile and probably need to be top 0.5% percentile in order to have a shot at competing at professional level in order to start making money.

In business, however, it is much more forgiving. In most market sectors, if you can be at the top 20% percentile with good marketing and brand strategies, you should be able to do well in most industries. But if you want to be the market leader, you would need to adopt a pro athlete mentally and be in the top 0.5% percentile in order to have a shot at dominating an industry.

One thing that I wished was that I had started entrepreneurship at 15 instead of in my 30s. That would give me a lot more time to fail, learn and a lot less financial burden as an adult. Also, I would suggest staying single while you are working on a new product venture if possible. Once you have a girlfriend/boyfriend, or get married, you will have a lot more obligations, spending, friction with your spouse, lack of money and time that you can provide them. You also will have less time to work on your startup, which ultimately will reduce your likelihood of succeeding.

The best scenario for a hardware entrepreneur is to achieve success before you are 35, so you can have some financial buffers and be able to provide a comfortable lifestyle for your loved ones instead of dragging them into your misery. If you are already in the later stage in your life, don't worry because chances are you have likely accumulated a lot more experience, insights, resources and connections that can be used to your advantage as well.

Start your venture the moment you believe you have a unique solution to a problem even if you don't have the resources to create it. You need to learn to be resourceful, move yourself to the area that will offer you the best chance of turning your solution into a reality. Reach out to anyone that you can learn from as much as possible and can be of help at the problem that you are solving. Even stopping by companies that can help you realize your solution, even though you can't afford their services. Gathering as much information as possible will naturally lead you to the next steps of actions to take and eventually get you closer to realizing your product. You will be amazed how much you can achieve with however little money you have if you have the confidence, right attitude and determination. That is all you need to open the right doors for you at the right time. As your venture progresses, you can leverage your progress with companies that need your solution or investors who believe in your vision to unlock more doors and resources that will help realize your product.

Practice, active learning, facing our fears, failing, analyzing our actions and improving our previous actions are the cycles anyone must go through to improve our chance of succeeding. It's through these cycles that we can find out your weaknesses, avoid future errors and improve our odds at succeeding at product ventures. So, when the right timing comes, you are ready to strike hard and succeed.

Remember, you can't learn to swim if you fear you will drown, you can't learn to drive if you are afraid you will get into a car crash. Trust yourself, you have everything to achieve the impossible when your actions are aligned with your goal.

Chapter 12

Big Idea & Hobbies

A great idea is probably the easiest part of entrepreneurship. It will improve your odds of success by a whopping 28%! I have a list of 400 plus innovative product ideas written down on my note pad, selecting the best one will take some thinking though.

Most times when you study the ideas that already turned startups into successful companies, you would realize that the same idea is probably applicable to different industries. For instance, when I first got started in the hobby of racing RC cars around 1997 with a 2 stroke nitro engine 1/10th scale on-road car that had a 2 speed transmission and can rip up to speeds of nearly 50mph. The high pitch screaming sound from the nitro engine is the closest feeling of driving a racing sports car down a race track. It was fun, addicting and exciting. However, the engine often is very tough to ignite and there could be many issues such as a burnt out glow plug, air and oil mixture not being right, a burnt crankshaft and the list just goes on. I would spend more time troubleshooting the engine than enjoying the excitement of my speedy RC car. Later on, I got two more race grade nitro engine RC cars and the reliability improved a lot. The engine would typically start within the first few tries. The high cost of the nitro fuel, the noise that drove my neighbors crazy, the grease and dirt that required constant cleaning, the often repairing and troubleshooting eventually drove me to my first electric brushless RC car in 2005. It was a game changer, my electric RC car got more run time than my nitro gas RC cars, faster take off speed, blazing top speed, rarely any troubleshooting required, no cleaning needed plus I can drive in the middle of the night without annoying the neighbors. Electric RC car had a clear advantage over the nitro gas RC car for every aspect, except the lack of heart pound loud engine noise. At that very moment, I was already thinking why are there not more electric cars on the road as that will mean no more oil changes, tune ups, changing of spark plugs, air filters, oil filters and much cheaper to drive. However, at the time, I wasn't in an entrepreneurship mindset, I was a fashion photographer and thought maybe when I have more money, I can toy with this idea. I am sure many people who are into the RC car hobby probably have similar revelations like me.

I am not here to discredit Elon Musk being the key person to popularize the electric car. What I am saying here is that anyone has a fair shot at coming up with great ideas, but only few have the right mindsets, the resourcefulness and the determination to turn big ideas into reality. What is more important is that one needs to have a consciousness that is one to two levels above the average person to be able to see the bigger picture. The ability to be able to see the bigger picture is what motivates massive action. What I saw at the time was that electric vehicles were a better all-around option to gas vehicles. What Elon Musk saw was "to accelerate the advent of sustainable transport by bringing compelling mass-market electric cars to market as soon as possible". The reason why Elon Musk pushed Tesla is very admirable thus, having many environmentally conscious individuals purchase his early product offerings, the $100,000 Roadster and snowballed into more product offerings. Based on the reports from "transportenvironment.org" electric cars at the moment produce in the range of 37% to 87% less CO2 than gasoline cars in the same class. The data is showing electric cars are significantly better for the climate than gasoline cars. However, the extraction of lithium, manganese, cobalt, graphite needed for the production of car batteries are very polluting for the environment as well since the soil, water and air will all be contaminated near these mining sites. No one knows the long term adverse effect of sudden massive increase in demand for mining these minerals, but we can be sure it will be quite bad for the people in the area that is being mined.

Current electric cars are definitely the right step towards a cleaner environment. But what if you are aware of the development of new solar powered cars like the Aptera that let you drive 40 mph per day all from the electricity generated from the solar panels alone and let you drive 1,000 miles on a single charge. Now, if you were to design a car that is best for our environment, would you go down the same path that Elon Musk did with Tesla, or the path of Aptera?

Now, what if you are aware of the development of "super capacitors" that can be fully charged in minutes, output more power than batteries for even faster acceleration, the capacity of charge will not degrade over time like batteries, so no need for expensive swapping of old car battery pack, much more environmentally friendly and much lighter weight and even better range efficiency. The last hurdle of super capacitors is solving the energy density issue and once that is solved, it will likely obsolete the need for lithium batteries for cars.

If you create an electric car that has twice the solar panel coverage than the Aptera with the windows and doors being solar panels, it should get you close to 80 mph range just on solar. Aptera uses Maxeon Gen 3 solar cells with a 23% efficiency. But what if you reach out to the National Renewable Energy Laboratory with their experimental solar cells at 39.5% efficiency which should offer you around a 140 mph mile range with just solar cells alone? Now, we replace the battery with the latest super capacitor, according to an article from "cleantechnica.com" Researchers at Bristol University and Surrey University in UK are claiming a 200+ mile range supercapacitor on the horizon. This ultimately gave us a truly off the grid electric vehicle with emission free 140 mph range for daily drives plus another 200+ mile range from the super capacitor.

Best of all, to fully charge the super capacitor only takes a few minutes, not hours like batteries.

Big ideas sometimes may seem far-fetched, but if your math is on point, it can be achievable, you just have to push beyond the limit. Oftentimes, techs that you need to complete big ideas are ready just a few years down the line. Big ideas are what we need for attracting early adopters and investors and often the strategy to finance the product development.

Nikola, a new hydrogen powered electric truck venture founded by Trevor Milton in 2015, tried to compete with Tesla. His big ideas of hydrogen powered electric trucks landed him massive investment and even went IPO without ever delivering a single vehicle to customers and Nikola was worth $34 billion in 2020. However, the founder Trevor Milton was found guilty in October of 2022 for felony on over exaggerating technology he never possessed to investors for funding and inflating his stock prices. He is now facing a sentence upward of 20 years.

Theranos, another big idea founded by Elizabeth Holmes in 2003 to revolutionize blood testing with just a few drops of blood, instead of tubes of blood needed for traditional blood testing. Her big idea landed her with over $700 million in venture money and over $10 billion valuation in 2013. However, investigators found that Elizabeth had none of the technology that she had claimed to have invented and therefore, Theranos was dissolved in 2018. She was found guilty in Jan 2022 and sentenced to 11 years and 3 months in jail.

There is a very fine line between big ideas and fraudulent acts. Big ideas that can be backed by technology that you or partners have developed and can be used for creating a working prototype is a great leverage that can propel your new venture to a billion dollar status.

Magic Leap, an AR technology company founded in 2010 by Rony Abovitz. His big idea enabled him to raise nearly $2 billion dollars from 2013 to 2017 without delivering a single product. In August of 2018, the Magic Leap 1 was finally released to the public with a hefty price tag of $2,300 and the reviews were mediocre, most people thought the Magic Leap was just hype. It took another 5 years and a total of $2.6 billion in funding. Magic Leap 2 was released on September 30th, 2022 and most reviews were putting it at the top of AR glasses. As you can see, if you have big ideas and enough proof of your technology to back up your claim, you can have as much as 13 years to improve your invention and won't be running into trouble with the law.

Another revelation that I had from the many years of RC car hobby was that RC cars can change the color and style of the car body by easily swapping the car body shell. I was always wondering why nobody designed a car that can swap out the body style easily, so people can change the style of their car from a sedan to a sports car and to a pickup whenever they like. This way, people can enjoy their car even more.

Recently, my wife got addicted to fishing since we have been living temporarily in a remote fishing town in Huizhou, China before moving back to San Francisco. I tag along sometime and she would be fishing and I try my best to write this book on my phone's notepad. What I noticed most of the days was that she didn't catch any fish, sometimes it's a few pinky sized fish, but never once a fish heavier than 1/2 pound. The whole time, I was hoping she would catch a couple of one pounders so we could make sea fish soup, however, of the 5 to 6 attempts, still no such luck yet. I never knew fishing was this tough, maybe we are at a fishing town that has been overfished. I chatted with fellows who were fishing nearby and was told there were big fishes in the area, but they have become very smart and rarely bite on the hooks, except for dumber small fishes. So, an idea came to mind. What if there is a mini boat the size of a spring water bottle with a see-through bottom for mounting a camera to position the baits precisely to where the big fishes are. The camera can also record all the actions and send the live-view back to the smartphone in real-time, so users can watch fishes biting the bait to add another level of excitement. The bottom of the boat has 2-3 anchoring points for fastening the hooks and each anchoring point is connected to a motor that spins slowly, so the bait will move through the water and look alive and be more attractive to large fishes. Then, add a fish-caller, a device that mimics the noise of small fish swimming through the water which will attract larger fishes that are hungry. Lastly, a small reservoir inside the boat that can release blood scented liquids to entice the fishes nearby to bite more frequently. Some fishing purists may say this takes out the fun of fishing, but I am sure many would love to come home after a long day of fishing with a few fish to make a warm bowl of soup.

Many of my new ideas are from issues that I dealt with in hobbies that I enjoy. Hobbies allows me to have an in-depth user experience and find out things that work well and things that need improvement. GoPro was discovered while the founder Nick Woodman was surfing and realized there is no camera designed for capturing the heroic photos of surfers. DJI started due to the founder's deep interest in flying aircrafts, which prompted him to develop a flight controller for RC helicopters as a school project during the years in Hong Kong University of Science & Technology. Both of these billion dollar business ideas came out of hobbies. So, don't brush off the importance of doing the things that you love during your off time. It's the perfect opportunity to dig deep into a subject matter in order to discover secrets that the average person would never realize. These secrets, or high levels of consciousness on a particular subject allows you to notice underlying problems that are hindering a group of users. The opportunity comes when you can conjure up a great solution to solve problems that users are facing and may not even be aware of.

Aside from hobbies, problems and issues that you face on a daily basis, problems you see on the news, new inventions that you see in magazines, industry trade shows are also sources that can help you come up with big ideas that can turn into great product ventures. Keep an open and curious mind. Ask questions when things are not working the way you thought it should. Play a constant game with your mind to find all the problems surrounding your life and identify the ones that you can excel at solving.

Here is a method that I often use to explore and quickly figure out whether an idea is worth exploring further. Once you have a product idea, you can draw out the solution that's on your mind on a piece of paper, no matter how bad your drawing skill is, this action turns your idea into a visible reality. Keep the drawing in a place where you can view it daily and snap a shot to store it on your smartphone homepage, so your mind can constantly think of a better version of the solution. Don't skim on drawing out your idea, it's the fastest and cheapest way to visually see your product come alive on paper, which is a very powerful first step toward realizing your product.

Keep on adding elements, features and functions to your product drawing to create the best solution possible. Don't hold back on the functions and features, keep adding them to your drawing, you can always take them out in case your engineering team tells you they are not possible. Keep revisiting your drawing for a week or so and repeat this process for other ideas that you have and compare them to find out which is the best product idea and most valuable solution that is missing in the market. This is a process that I use to decide on what product to tackle next.

Another deciding factor for me is whether the project is fun for me. I am the type of person that can't focus on solving a problem that I am not passionate about. The last thing that I want is to spend the next 10-20 years of my life on a product venture that I don't really care for except for a chance to chase the money. My friend, Aaron Silverberg of Talo toothbrush offered me a 50% stake in his toothbrush venture right around the time I was developing IDOLCAM. I know it's a great product and very innovative design, plus everyone needs a better toothbrush. Even though, it's a compelling product, I am just not that passionate about a toothbrush as Aaron was, so I turned down the offer and continued with the IDOLCAM venture. But we did agree to create a product together one day, maybe a flying car.

Chapter 13

Tactics & Strategies

For any hardware creator and entrepreneur wanting to succeed in today's competitive business environments, they must have a set of tactics that will help them move toward the next milestone, so their startups can survive and thrive. We, as hardware creators, also need strategies, so the value of our product is superior to our competitors leading the consumers to choose our product over others.

Both tactics and strategies are pre-calculated actions with a desired goal in mind. Every action in a business likely falls into either a tactic or efforts towards a strategy. For example, I didn't, all of a sudden, decide to spend hundreds of hours writing this book. Writing "Hardware Billionaire" is part of both a tactic and a strategy for IDOLCAM. The first reason why I decided to write this book was while I began working on IDOLCAM in 2016, I wasn't able to find too much information on how someone can create a world class electronic product with a very tight budget. So, my gut feeling is telling me that the market needs an in-depth book on how someone with enough determination can turn their dream product into reality. With my experience in the hardware creation business and my very tight budget, I knew I was the best person to write this book. Secondly, I had already sold out all the IDOLCAM units until I got further funding from investors. I needed another stream of income and I hope this book can help pay for some of the expenses so I can focus more of my time on meeting investors and not working on side gigs to pay bills. Thirdly, this book will be a gift for every investor that I meet and it will provide a lot more insight into what I have done so far with IDOLCAM and allow them learn more about the way I think. I also believe this book will greatly increase my chance of landing investment than with just a PPT and a brief 5 minute presentation. The fourth reason would be, the more copies of "Hardware Billionaire" that I sell, the more people will know about IDOLCAM, so when IDOLCAM V2 is in production, many more people would have been aware of the IDOLCAM and would be ready to buy. The fifth reason is that this book will increase brand recognition for IDOLCAM. Lastly, this is a great way to document the IDOLCAM journey and I can look back years later and be proud of what I had accomplished and where I could improve on.

Tactics and strategies will vary greatly for each hardware creator. You may be lacking funding, or lacking product development skills, maybe you need to beat your competitors to the market with your new product launch, or build a working prototype to prove to investors that you have what it takes, or find ways to reduce your burn rate and the list just goes on. Since the obstacles are very different from creator to creator, your tactics and strategies also need to be different in order to reach your milestone.

So, first you need to identify the next 3 to 5 most crucial tactical steps that you need to take in order to get your startup to the next milestone. Once you define the goals of these tactical steps, then you have to reverse engineer the list of things that you need to do in order to achieve the outcomes you have in mind. Of course, not all tactics and strategies will pan out the way you envisioned them, you may need to do a lot of testing and adjustment in order to achieve the desired effects.

Typically, tactics are short term actions with immediate results, such as building a MVP prototype in one month to show to investors, run short sales to drive up revenue, apply for patents to protect your product, find a great manufacturer so you can efficiently build your products.

While strategies are typically actions that you need to repeat over a long period of time to achieve desired effect, some of these strategies are trying to be known as the most innovative product company, being known as the lowest priced or most premium priced product in your category, or being known as the longest warranty, or even the easiest to use product in your category. Strategy can also be ways to increase your manufacturing efficiency, so you can sell at lower prices than your competitor, similar to what Tesla is doing with electric cars and Xiaomi with smartphones.

Strategy can also be a marketing channel or method that you have mastered. Strategies can sometimes be used in a combination of strategies and tactics stacked together for the best results.

To put it simply, tactics are short term actions that are used by creators to gain an upper hand in the marketing ventures to make their products look unique or mostly preferable. They are typically tricks or games applied to make buyers take desired actions that are not the most beneficial for them. Thus, tactics are not sustainable actions for the long run. While strategies are good genuine deeds the creators try to provide for buyers and this will build karma points over time, but it may take years to see the result.

Unfortunately, I won't be able to give you the exact tactics and strategies that you need for your product startup, but at least I will make you aware of the importance and better understand the difference between the two.

Chapter 14

Spirituality & Health

We are living in a world of energy, everything that we can see, touch, our feelings, thoughts and mental state are all made up of energy vibrating at different frequencies. Energy attracts more energy vibrating at a similar frequency. That's why happy people attract more happy people, sad and depressed people attract more sad and depressed people, and successful people attract more successful people into their orbits. It's why entrepreneurs usually know more entrepreneurs, basketball players will know a few basketball players in their circle. The thoughts and energy that we unconsciously emit is what created our current reality. That's why it's really important to monitor the underlying feelings and thoughts that your mind is emitting. You want to analyze the energy that your mind is emitting, whether it is mostly positive, or negative, fear, or hope? Once you are aware of the dominant energy your mind is emitting, you can consciously make an effort to shift your mental state toward a more positive one and start to emit more positive energy frequencies, which will attract more positive people, things and events into your world.

Optimism is really the only thing an entrepreneur has initially to get a project started. It helps them push through all obstacles and curveballs during the development process. That's why if you want the best chance at creating a product with very limited resources, you have to be very optimistic and conscious of the energy that you are emitting, it should be full of positivity and hope. Because you may not see any financial awards for years until your product is ready for market and it is only when your product is desired by the market that you can get rewarded. You have to be aware of the energy flowing around you and it has to be positive, not negative. If you are generally a positive person, but you are surrounded by naysayers daily, eventually your mind and energy will slowly shift toward the same mindset and frequency of naysayers. So, be aware of the energy that you are emitting and the energy that surrounds you because your reality is the sum of all the energies you have whether consciously or not.

Since our mind emits frequencies and frequencies are energies and energies turn into action and actions have the power to transform ideas into reality. As entrepreneurs, we want to focus our minds on the frequency of the product that we want to create and over time by focusing our energy on our product idea, eventually our idea can turn into a real product. For me, that's how I turned ideas like the 6 ft helicam, 20 lb hexacopters, Hollywood gimbal and IDOLCAM from vague ideas into action, then tangible prototypes and lastly functional products. These are products I never believed that I could create if you had asked me in my 20s.

Although creating hardware products is a shot at becoming rich and famous, however, it is only half the game. The ultimate goal in life is achieving true harmony with oneself. A resistance and conflict free inner and outer self where everything you think and act are in unison. Your mind and heart is calm as the early summer breeze in the middle of a pond when faced with the utmost adversity. Nothing in the world can stop you in the path of growing as a person and improving as an entrepreneur. All the chaos, mishaps, scares and failures are just great stories and journeys that you must embark on in order to succeed and enrich your legacy. Through these extraordinary experiences are what makes your legacy exciting and your life here on earth worthwhile.

When your mind and action are in unison, you are not swimming upstream, beating yourself over every little mistake, bitter about the limited resources that you have, fearing the failures of tomorrow and freeing yourself from these energy robbing doubts that can cripple you from advancing. Too many of us are wasting our lives on the fear of "what if." The lack of believing in yourself robs you of the great potential that you have within and ultimately falls short of what you can truly become.

The longer I practice entrepreneurship, the more I realize the importance of a positive mindset and confidence in oneself is really the fundamental difference between success and failure. Without a calm and peaceful mindset, anyone in their right mind would wilt under the tremendous pressure of entrepreneurship.

I should have given up on IDOLCAM a few years ago, or should have never started it in the first place, but the optimism and belief I had turned a very complex idea into reality and it's the faith that helped me keep the project alive.

There are just too many practical reasons to just live out a normal life and follow the safe steps that society has laid out for us. Many people in their late thirties and early forties are starting to have panic attacks and depression, even though they have already achieved the American dream of owning a nice house, fancy car and a family. I am not a psychologist, but I believe too many people have spent their lives busy building a facade to let others know that they are doing well from the outside, but have neglected far too long to what they truly wanted for themselves on the inside.

If you take a big step backward and view life in a 3rd person point of view, you will realize a life living safely is a life merely repeating yesterday over and over again. I believe we all have our purposes here on earth and everyone's mission will be different. It is just wasteful to not live out to one's true potential and accept to be the average.

Entrepreneurship is a lifetime journey, it's okay to be the turtle, just make sure your compass is calibrated and your helm is steered to the right direction.

One overlooked aspect for entrepreneurs is health. Not only do entrepreneurs need to be healthy, you should be fit like an athlete. Poor diet, lack of sleep, no exercise may seem like the lifestyle of a true entrepreneur. Imagine you get 5 hours of sleep every day and eat fast food daily and no time for exercise, chances are over time you will develop high blood pressure, cholesterol and risk of stroke and heart attack. If your mind is probably foggy most of the time, it means you have high chances of making poor decisions in critical times. If you are an investor, or employee, would you bet on a founder with poor health habits, or someone who is healthy like a tiger?

Founders with poor health habits are a liability to the company. It's like getting on a small airplane greeted by a 300 lb pilot who huffs and puffs as he climbs up the stairs to the cockpit, the odds are against you before you take a flight. So, make it a priority to get in shape, eat and sleep well. It's a shame to make it big in hardware entrepreneurship, but end up spending life on a hospital bed paid with the money you work so hard to get.

Chapter 15

The Next Hardware Billionaire

Entrepreneurship can't guarantee your wealth and fame, but it's a great method for people who are not from wealthy families to have a shot at becoming wealthy. The experience of running a hardware business will definitely make you a stronger and wiser person.

To become a hardware billionaire, first I am not one myself, nor anywhere close to it, so just take it with a grain of salt. But I do believe anyone wanting a shot at becoming a hardware billionaire would first be a huge dreamer and believer. Discipline, persistence, good work ethics are just prerequisites. To run a hardware company worth billions, for one you will need an amazing product that is highly desired by the market, unique and not easily replaced. Second, you will need an amazing creative team that can tell a captivating story of your product. Thirdly, you need a marketing team that understands how to leverage PR and influencers material for the highest ROI marketing/advertising campaigns. Fourthly, a seamless production and delivery of the products to customers. Lastly, a mature omni channel distribution network and a trustworthy brand are the foundations that are needed to build a hardware product company that can worth billions.

The chance of building a billion dollar hardware company is slim, but anyone embarking on a venture in hardware products should have the same attitude and determination as if you are building a unicorn. So, even if you fall short, it will at least be worth a lot more than if you aimed low.

My suggestion is don't look at it as a mountainous task, but as a passion, an art form and a lifestyle that you will spend your life living, breathing and mastering it.

Chapter 16

Final Words

To all the brave souls that have been reading up to this point, I hope it has been worth your precious time. I also hope that one day I will come back with a version 2 of "Hardware Billionaires" to walk you through all the steps that I took to achieve billionaire status. I truly believe IDOLCAM is my vehicle to billions, but of course I will need a lot of luck, great timing, smart decision and investors to provide us the funds to run my money printing machine, IDOLCAM and keep the bills printing in my sleep.

But I truly believe the hidden treasure in entrepreneurship is not the money, but rather you will realize your true potential honing the power and confidence to turn any ideas into products that can propel the world forward.

I wish you all a rewarding hardware venture and feel free to write to me with your suggestions and inputs to support@idolcam.co. I hope everyone has a great life, enjoys the process and makes a whole lot of money doing hardware. But most importantly, keep on learning, get wiser along the way and live a peaceful and fulfilling life.

I want to leave a few last words of wisdom that I have gathered along the way. These words have helped me to keep on marching forward in peace and confidence.

"Let flowers be flowers, let trees be trees and let you be yourself."

"Far too many lions turn cats, redwood trees turn bonsai and genius turn lawyers and doctors."

"A smart person would study so he/she can get good grades, go to a good university, get a good job, make good money, buy a car and a house. This process is a long one and it's painful to reach these societal goals and find no happy ending. A wise person would study for the love of studying, go to university for the love of knowledge, work at a job that he loves and every part of his/her life is full of fun and enjoyment with no expectation."

Now is your turn to choose the life you want to live and I hope it's a wise one and one that you would enjoy with no regrets.

Thank you for finishing my first book, Hardware Billionaires!

Jason Lam

IDOLCAM Founder

无畏,

无常,

当下,

一心.

No Fear, Accept Changes, At Present, One Heart.

Peace & Love!

The End.

Get "Hardware Billionaires" book at,

https://www.idolcam.co/hardwarebillionaires.html

Signup for IDOLCAM V2 launch,

https://www.idolcam.co

www.ingramcontent.com/pod-product-compliance
Lightning Source LLC
Chambersburg PA
CBHW050732010526
44107CB00010B/827